# Influential Rapport

Influence and Persuade in Work, Life and Leisure

By
## James M. Seetoo

SNLP Licensed Trainer NLP
SNLP Licensed Coaching Trainer
ICBCH Hypnosis Trainer
Hogan Assessments Certified Practitioner

Influential Rapport

Influence and Persuade in Work, Life and Leisure

James M. Seetoo

Copyright © 2020 James M. Seetoo

All Rights Reserved.

All rights reserved. No part of this publication may be reproduced, distributed, or transmitted in any form or by any means, including photocopying, recording, or other electronic or mechanical methods, without the prior written permission from the author, except in the case of brief quotations embodied in critical reviews and certain other non-commercial uses permitted by copyright law.

First Printing:

ISBN: 978-1-7356373-1-0

# Why Read This Book?

The ability to create rapport and powerful connections to influence and persuade is a critical skillset in building strong relationships in both your personal and professional life. By using the tools in this book, you will understand the dynamics of Rapport, how you are influenced by them and how you can use them to influence others. Persuasion is the art of bringing others to your point of view. You can do this by bludgeoning the other person or by showing them how their interests and yours align, thereby making it their idea to work with you to a common goal that happens to be the one you have set out for them.

Rapport is a natural phenomenon that was necessary for the survival of our species. As much as someone might be a loner, there is still a need to be able to interact with others in order to maneuver through society successfully. But similar to playing a sport, some play for fun and those who play professionally. This book will show you to be a professional in the skills of influence and persuasion, leveraging rapport.

Persuasion and influence can be achieved outside of creating rapport, but when you have the ability to leverage this tool that is inherent in all of us, you will be able to more closely align with others, understand what motivates them, how they maybe trying to manipulate you, and create partners rather than adversaries to create the life you want.

# About This Book

The books is separated into two sections. The first outlines the concepts behind the 7 levels of rapport, what they are and how they are used when interacting with people. The second illustrates these concepts and their use in more detail using the fictional story of Drew, a character whose journey embodies the 7 levels of rapport.

This section also includes exercises for sharpening your own skills using Influential Rapport. Additional exercises can be found at: www.influentualrapport.com.

# About the Author

James M. Seetoo is the author of the bestselling book *The 5 Keys To Hypnotic Selling* and has applied the skills of influence and persuasion as taught in neuro-linguistic programming (NLP) and hypnosis. He first held a successful career in the executive recruiting industry and with that wealth of experience, transitioned into corporate training and coaching executives and others in sales, management, NLP and hypnosis.

James has delivered training domestically and internationally in countries such as Israel and Costa Rica. He has proven that his skill sets are transferable to industries as diverse as biotechnology, pharmaceutical, high tech, intellectual property, finance, the construction industry and executive search and recruitment proved by clients having increased their sales to seven figures.

Please find more information at https://jc2consulting.com.

# Table of Contents

Chapter 1 What is Rapport and Why You Want It ............ 1

Chapter 2 What Can You Do with Rapport? ................. 10

Chapter 3 The Rapport Process ............................ 13

Chapter 4 Rapport Level 1 - Awareness ................... 17

Chapter 5 Rapport Level 2 – Attention ................... 21

Chapter 6 Rapport Level 3 - Respect ..................... 24

Chapter 7 Rapport Level 4 – Trust ....................... 28

Chapter 8 Rapport Level 5 - Affiliation ................. 33

Chapter 9 Rapport Level 6 – Identification .............. 37

Chapter 10 Rapport Level 7 – Love ....................... 41

Chapter 11 How to Gain Rapport .......................... 46

Chapter 12 Leveraging Rapport ........................... 58

Chapter 13 Trust ........................................ 68

Chapter 14 Level 6 – Identification = Affinity/Affiliation/Admiration/Affection ............ 73

Chapter 15 Level 7 – Love ............................... 81

Chapter 16 What Got You Here Will Keep You Here ......... 90

Chapter 17 Bringing It All Together ..................... 99

Chapter 18 Quick Start Guide ............................ 107

Chapter 19 Final Thoughts ............................... 114

# Chapter 1
# What is Rapport and Why You Want It

It is a terrible thing to be alone in a crowd. When it seems everyone around you has a companion, a partner, a group of friends, or a tribe and you are on the outside looking in, observing things that others don't seem to. For some reason, however, you are not noticed, not connected, and not connecting.

You are tied into your own thoughts and feelings, and many times you intuitively know what others are likely feeling, and yet that spark, that connection that others seem to have, eludes you. Maybe at a party you end up leaning against a wall hoping that someone will approach you. Worse, perhaps you have given up on going to parties because, at some point, that lack of interaction is too much to bear. After all, that elusive ingredient doesn't seem to be there for you.

A spark can light a fire trail leading to connection, friendship, fellowship, camaraderie, and even love – all of which are results of rapport.

Rapport is not about liking someone, although it can definitely lead to that. Rapport is about being on the same wavelength and communicating at an auditory, visual, even tactile or kinesthetic level, ultimately moving one towards a multiphasic structure that is flexible and yet also directed. Learning rapport is the first step in moving towards is an omnichannel communication strategy between the persuader and their audience.

The question might be asked, why are we setting up a system? Isn't it enough to have vivid images and great information when speaking with individuals and audiences? After all the great communicators are the ones presenting compelling information regardless of whether it is news, entertainment, or propaganda. What most people don't realize is that what they are viewing is the end result of a structured presentation that bypasses the critical factor, that aspect of the conscious mind that is busy running an internal dialogue, and engrosses the individual in either a new way of experiencing the world or even more powerfully enhances that person's already existing point of view. When that happens, it is only a matter of directing the investment that the person has made in their points of view to get moving in the direction the persuader wants.

Rapport becomes the first step in the process of persuasion. It is the first phase in the multiphasic system of rapport building to influence and persuade.

**Misconceptions About the Concept of Rapport**

When you think about rapport, the first misconception about it is about people who like each other and have easy, free-flowing communication. It doesn't actually have anything to do with liking the other person, although generally, it leads to respect, and often leads to friendship and more.

The second common misconception is that rapport is random, and it is this second misconception that is the most profound and influential.

When people connect across different languages and cultures, there are unconscious processes that influence the creation of rapport. And even though these are happening outside of conscious awareness, it doesn't mean that it happens by chance. By learning specific skills, you will be able to leverage this phenomenon and create the conditions to influence and persuade in every situation.

*Influential Rapport*

So, let's define the concept of rapport. The Merriam-Webster Dictionary defines rapport as "a relationship characterized by agreement, mutual understanding, or empathy that makes communication possible or easy." For our purposes, this is a useful definition that leaves out an explicit emphasis on liking the other person or people. The part I which to emphasize is <u>mutual understanding</u> because that is a much more useful definition of the function of rapport.

When I was younger, I was a member of one of New York City's first hardcore punk bands, and like the majority of people in the scene, we had *our* clubs. When you think of people in the hardcore punk scene, the things that come to mind, other than loud music, may be the leather jackets, bondage clothing, piercings, and ripped shirts – basically all part of being a member of a scene. It is very much like fans of a sports team wearing team colors and jerseys or, in more extreme cases, gang colors. Oddly enough, in the punk scene, there was an emphasis on non-conformity, and yet everyone was wearing the same thing. This different yet similar fashion style was a sign of rapport blazing in the night like a bonfire. After a while, I decided to go a different route and donned brightly colored button-down shirts, tailored blazers, a thirties era fedora, and carried a walking stick. Even then, I was accepted but not because of the status of being in a band, but because I quickly built a rapport with people and was able to leverage that with new people. I wasn't a bizarre, out-of-place stranger in a pogo dancing mosh pit.

One weekday night, I was hanging out at one of our regular clubs when I was approached by an older, bearded guy with long hair. He wasn't exactly a punk stereotype, but maybe that's why he decided to talk to me. He began by asking me questions about why I was there. I would say he was a bit guarded, and me being Asian, there weren't many Asians in the punk clubs back then. When he discovered I played in the band at this club, he began to relax. He introduced himself as Bill and then started a long conversation about martial arts. It turned out he was really into the martial arts, and this conversation turned into a three-hour discussion with a guy who, despite his tough appearance, was very educated. We enjoyed a lot of similar points of view.

He capped off the conversation by insisting on giving me a present. He pulled out a large clasp knife with a saw tooth blade that appeared to have had hard use and left. He went downstairs and pulled out of the club on a large Harley Davidson motorcycle. I went to get a drink, and the bartender looked at me with shock saying, "I can't believe it." When I asked why he stated that I had just spent the last three hours chatting with Wild Bill.

"What do you mean?" I enquired.

"He's crazy," the bartender declared. "Even the others in the motorcycle gang are afraid of Wild Bill and don't hang out with him. He pretty much drives everybody he talks to away."

"Seemed like a pretty nice guy," I replied.

Once I returned home, I got a good look at the knife he had given me and noticed it had a lot of rust-colored, dried stains on the blade. Perhaps the bartender might have had a point.

What is the difference between being a part of a crowd and blending in, being able to stand out, being totally different, and even come away with a somewhat questionable gift from someone who has a history of being antisocial at best?

It is the ability to create rapport.

My encounter with Wild Bill makes for a great story, and at the same time, it is a perfect illustration of what can happen when you have the skill to create rapport. In this case, it led to a fascinating conversation with someone who was not exactly known for having conversations with people outside of their motorcycle club, and apparently not even there. Did I approach the discussion with the idea of getting something? Not particularly. In fact, I didn't really have an agenda other than to discover what this fellow was all about while not getting into a potentially tricky or nasty situation.

By creating rapport, I was able to draw him out of that public persona that he typically showed the world and connected with the person behind it. This led to a memorable interaction.

When building rapport, you begin to affect the most crucial part of the influence and persuasion process: gaining and holding the other person's attention. There are a lot of ways to gain attention, and we see it all the time on social media: people doing incredibly stupid things like eating laundry detergent pods or riding shopping carts into walls. Other than a momentary reaction or ten minutes of fame, these actions don't hold a person's attention to the point where it would influence that other person in a positive way.

Rapport implies an exchange with other people, a sharing of ideas, emotions, and attitudes, among many things shared on multiple levels, both conscious and unconscious, in one-on-one or group situations.

By understanding how to gain rapport with others, you can create connections with people from various backgrounds and beliefs that can lead to rewarding relationships regardless of whether you agree on issues or not. A deep rapport allows both parties to respect the other person's ideas and feelings at a profound level without requiring agreement or acquiescence.

Leveraging the skill of gaining and deepening rapport will lead to healthy relationships in your personal and professional life. It will give you the ability and confidence to connect, influence, and persuade in any situation.

I remember when I began genuinely putting these skills into practice. I had used them previously when I had my company in Yugoslavia, and they seemed to help smooth interactions with people. Still, it is hard to say that other than making people more at ease with dealing with me, that they allowed me to influence and persuade during deals. Looking back on it, I am sure the effect was positive but diluted.

With the dissolution of Yugoslavia, the business imploded. Subsequently, I was invited to join an executive search firm by a friend already working there. This type of search firm operated in areas that were new to me: medical devices, specialty chemicals, and different kinds of manufacturing as well as supply chain. These were out of my realm of experience as an English major. I had previously worked on building a company with my best friend and brother, sourcing deals and commodities in a very different country and culture. This new company, a boutique search firm, allowed quite a bit of leeway in how one went about finding people. It nevertheless focused; however, on getting people to listen and selling them on exploring new opportunities while at the same time selling corporate clients on the candidates.

At first, my friend invited me to shadow him; he had been doing this type of business successfully for several years. He was always entertaining on the phone. Not so much for his ability to influence and persuade – well, I suppose for lack of a better word he was good at deceiving people. I soon realized that he would pretty much say whatever it took to get a person to become interested in making a career move. The truth was a distant and very secondary consideration. His approach was neither encouraged nor approved by the company's partners, who were all very ethical. One of the partners served as a mentor to me, and to this day, I am in touch with him even though he's long been retired.

Quickly realizing I couldn't operate the way my friend was I knew I would have to find my own method. Reviewing the skills I had started learning on my journey into international trade, I dove deeply into the skills of neurolinguistic programming (NLP) and hypnosis.

I sought out training in different areas of rapport, influence, and persuasion. I concentrated on finding people who were using these skill sets in the real world.

Many people reason that these skills are only useful in therapeutic situations and thinking in a very siloed way. After all, at the heart of it, effective therapy revolves around getting someone to believe and accept new methods in order to solve old problems. They're guided into embracing "Not this" (their problem) but "this" (their desired solution). And it is the same thing when it comes to effective influence and persuasion. The basis of it all is rapport. Without the ability to get and hold another person's or audience's attention, you can say the most brilliant thing ever, and there won't be anyone listening much less accepting what you have to say.

It took a few weeks, but I didn't want to keep dialing for dollars, cold calling, and getting hung up on, so I worked on a few skills that I could use quickly, and the day came when I decided I would make calls differently than I had before.

The first person I called was the president of a company. I remember this vividly because my hands were shaking when I was dialing his number, and I had to stand up because my nerves wouldn't let me sit still. I called around lunchtime, thinking I would leave him a message, he was my first call and felt that I ease myself in with a warm-up call.

Like some best-laid plans, this one didn't go the way I thought it would. On the second ring, the president of this company picked up the phone, and I had no choice but to start talking with him using the new skills I had been practicing. The thought stuck in my mind that he would call me out on what I was doing and hang up. It didn't go that way either. We connected. Our conversation went far longer and was more profound than the average recruiting discussions that I had been having, and we ended up staying on the call for over forty-five minutes. It was challenging getting him off the phone. When I eventually hung up, I couldn't believe how well the call went, I sat back reviewing what had just happened, shocked at how natural the conversation had been.

Then I did it again and again and again. Now it is second nature to me and has been the key to building a very successful practice that has branched out into coaching, sales training, and licensing NLP practitioners, master practitioners, and certifying hypnotists.

Using the rapport skills taught in NLP has taken the randomness out of my interactions with others. That chance connection I had with someone I just met became a common occurrence. All it took was understanding the things that I sometimes did successfully already unconsciously, learn to use them consciously, and then practice them until I did them automatically all the time.

This book will lay it all out for you by explaining what is going on and the type of effect you have on others when you learn a few simple skills and how to incorporate them into your life easily. All you have to do is commit to reading through the book, play with each skill separately, and soon, they will start to blend and become the way you communicate.

There are secrets I know, and by continuing to read, you will too. You are invited to come on this journey that will present you the skills to make more money, build better relationships, and have more time to enjoy them. By embracing them, you'll develop the ability to create a connected life.

# Chapter 2

# What Can You Do with Rapport?

I am often asked the question: "What can you do with rapport?" It seems to me that this would be a way of trying to define the limits of the skill sets rather than extend the boundaries. I can certainly understand this mindset. We live in a culture where the side mirrors on American vehicles are required to be engraved with the phrase "objects in mirror are closer than they appear" as a safety feature. We're used to wanting to know boundaries. It is something that we are taught in school, in sports, and society, and these boundaries serve a real purpose.

When you have the skills of quickly building and maintaining rapport, you get to set the boundaries, rather than having them fixed for you. In every interaction, there are boundaries, and depending on the situation, they can be strict and inhibit your ability to influence and persuade. For example, at work, you have to be careful about discussing politics, religion, or commenting on someone who is wearing something nice or has changed their hairstyle.

That being said, when you have rapport and have built a relationship, those boundaries are not nearly as hard and fast as for those who you have just met. I have found that in my interactions, the language, topics, and humor used when speaking with friends is vastly different than what is used with others. Language, topics, and humor are often different when speaking with parents, distant relatives, acquaintances, people you have just met, the boss, co-workers, and people one is interacting with on a transactional basis such as a server or doctor.

Exceptions prove the rule because bartenders and hair stylists, for example, seem to be in a different category. Possibly this is because alcohol is involved, and with hairstylists because they want to know your goal when asking for a new style, and this means personal sharing.

Usually described as a good listener, I think that might have been one of my main talents already as a child. I was inclined to listen much more than talk. That could also be a trait of being a middle child as they are more likely to be the peacemaker of the family, as described by author Katrin Schumann in her book, *The Secret Powers of Middle Children*. In order to do that, it became second nature to observe and absorb information rather than offering an opinion first.

Not offering an immediate opinion can naturally lead to others mistaking the middle child's tendency to listen as interest when it is in reality often a more of not knowing how to extricate themselves from a conversation. Combine that with being raised to have good manners, and you get stuck being the go-to person when someone wants to unload their problems. You only have three choices at that point: be rude (not something I was raised to do), fall asleep in front of them, or listen. It is in the listening that I began to learn how to influence and persuade using the rapport I had inadvertently created.

When you are able to create rapport, you will get people talking about things that they only usually tell people with whom they are incredibly close and sometimes not even then. Therapists rely on this phenomenon, explaining that it is sometimes easier to tell a stranger things than you can your friends because of the fear of embarrassment. While this is true, many therapists fail to create rapport, so they rely on the "stranger" aspect and their status as a therapist rather than being able to draw the other person out.

Since this is not a book about therapy, I will show you how to draw people out with rapport, and you will then be able to influence, persuade and offer alternatives to them if you are helping them with their problem. You can have better interactions, better relationships, better friendships, and a better life when you have rapport because when you are able to create rapport with others, you will find you can have a better rapport with yourself.

# Chapter 3

# The Rapport Process

Leveraging rapport involves understanding several levels of rapport and the nuances involved in each of them. While you want to have rapport in all your interactions, you don't want to spend time and resourcescreating deep connections when they are neither necessary nor desirable. Building a sense of "just enough" rapport will allow you to have the skill to influence people rather than bludgeoning them into compliance. It will also allow you to protect yourself from creating rapport when it isn't desirable.

Many women will be very aware of non-desirable rapport due to the unfortunate phenomenon of stalking, which seems more prevalent due to people having more touchpoints via social media, online presence, and information availability. An innocent interaction where a small bit of rapport can be misinterpreted into indicators of interest can be blown up to massive proportions in the minds of some individuals.

Let me say right now that you are not responsible for the workings of the mentally ill mind and that a person's reaction to the way they move through the world is their sole responsibility. I am a strong advocate for protecting oneself at all times, and I believe in vigorous self-defense, both verbal and physical.

This is where the concept of good manners has developed over time in society. Good manners are a way of codifying acceptable behavior, and because we have seen an erosion of this in our society over the years, even good manners can be mistaken for indicators of interest. At the risk of sounding old fashioned, good manners are an elemental component when building rapport because they are a sign of respect for the other person. On an unconscious level, you are setting expectations for how you expect to be treated.

Now that I have warned you of some of the possible pitfalls of rapport, being in control of the process involves an awareness that it is a process. Yes, rapport can seem instantaneous at times, and I will be sharing techniques to speed up the process. Still, there's an old saying that is applied in martial arts and gun handling: "slow is smooth, and smooth is fast." In other words, get good at the process, and then the process will be seamless.

In order to make it seamless, the first step is understanding the stages and levels of rapport.

Levels of Rapport – Please insert graphic

- Awareness
- Attention
- Respect
- Trust
- Affiliation - Affinity/Affection/Admiration/Authority
- Identification
- Love

When talking about the rapport process and these levels of rapport, every interaction begins and ends with some level of rapport. Know what level your interaction is operating on and how to move a person through the different levels determines the kind of interaction that you have with that person. At the initial levels of rapport, interactions are often transactional. For example, when you check in your luggage at the airport, especially these days with kiosk type check in, you're interacting with a machine for the majority of the time. By the time you get to the an actual person, you've already entered your information and even put your own luggage tags on your bags so the

*Influential Rapport*

only interaction you have with a person involves making sure that you put your luggage on a conveyor belt properly. Hardly a great customer experience and it is totally transactional.

A different example would be when you arrive a the airport and interact with a person who checks you in, talks to you by name and also is able to provide useful information when asked. This is a person with whom you can build rapport. By speaking with that person as a person, even to the extent of talking about how that person's day is going and having a pleasant transaction, you're building rapport.

I remember one time when I was booked on a flight to Orlando, Florida and went up to the ticket agent to check in. I was in a good mood because I had left plenty of time to make my flight and so wasn't in a rush. She noticed that I was in a good mood and I mentioned that I was nice and relaxed because I had left a lot of time to make the flight. I asked her how her day was going and we went on to talk about how busy she had been earlier with canceled flights and irate passengers and how happy she was to have at least one customer who wasn't mad about something.

We had a very pleasant interaction and I casually asked if any upgrades were available. She smiled and said, just a second and looked back at her computer, typing a very long string of numbers. At this time I didn't have a lot of member reward points or any other special status but she went out of her way to look for me. She asked for my boarding pass back and handed me a new one that said, First Class on it. I took it and told her, "You made my day," and she replied, "You made mine just by being in a good mood."

What started out as a very transactional interaction quickly went into something much better and more meaningful and there is defined process to go from a very basic level of rapport to one that will not only allow you a much deeper level of connection but one that will also allow you to leverage that connection with other people to influence and persuade and in this case, we went from Awareness to Respect very quickly. The next chapter will have more details about how to go about doing this and as we go farther into the book, you'll learn how each of the rapport levels builds on the next.

At this point it's important to note that this is a dynamic process and that movement is not always one way from a lower level of rapport to a higher one. Rather, the process often shifts back and forth until it finds the right level for the interaction and when these interactions become regular such as a working or social environment then the base levels tend to be higher to begin with. In other words, once you have rapport the last level you had in your interaction with a person tends to be the beginning level in your next encounter with that person. But context can change the level of rapport in your next interaction and sometimes it makes sense to lower that level depending on the situation. Developing the ability to move a person through the different levels will give you greater range in your ability to persuade and influence using rapport.

Think about your best conversations with close friends. They start out in one place, then seemingly on their own they move to another and then another and the topics often shift from serious to funny to philosophical to practical and back to serious or funny etc. These changes don't break rapport but the level of rapport flexes to fit the interaction naturally. That feeling of comfort in the relationship is rapport.

# Chapter 4
# Rapport Level 1 - Awareness

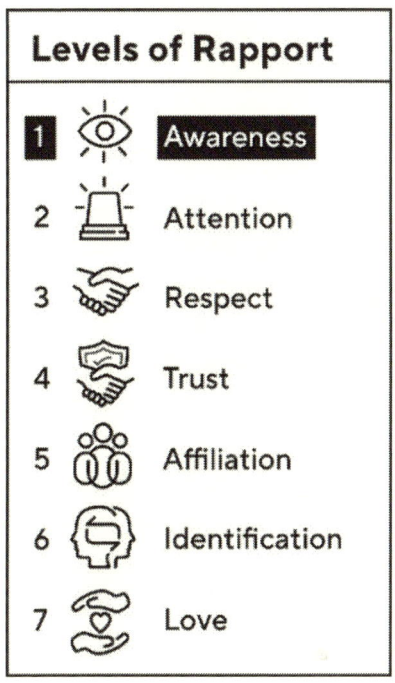

The first and most important of these levels of rapport is awareness. For you to have rapport with another person, that person has to know that you exist and that you deserve their notice. At the same time, if you spend all your time in your head and other people don't exist for you, then you are in no position to create rapport with anyone, much less build a deep relationship.

Does this mean talking loudly, waving your arms, and being a dog and pony show to get peoples' awareness? You could do that, but it is likely not the way to gain any sort of rapport that will lead to a situation that could provide an opportunity to influence and persuade and will probably have minimal entertainment value for anyone. Even if it has some level of entertainment value, it will have to lead to an escalating series of antics because, over time, it will lose impact for you and everyone else. There is a reason why the *Jackass* series of movies lost their popularity. After a while, people became numb to the antics, and soon their interest shifted to other entertaining films.

Having awareness is very much like a moment that happened while I was driving down a small road near my home. A residential area, I was driving around thirty-five miles an hour. Off to my right and about 300 feet in front of me, I became *aware* of something moving. A doe poked her head out from behind some bushes, and she walked out onto the road, followed by three fawns. Did I become aware of them? Absolutely, and then I immediately slowed down, judging that by doing so, they would likely have crossed the road before I got to that point. Still, I was by no means certain they were actually aware of me because the doe seemed to be focusing on the other side of the road, and the fawns were focused on their mother.

To gain, build, and leverage rapport into influence and persuasion *awareness* must be mutual; this is the beginning of the rapport process. One way awareness can be frustrating; however, is if it persists and is not welcome, it can then be classified as infatuation, which can lead to obsession.

The ability to become aware involves understanding the filters erected in our minds so that we could function in the world. The human body sends 11 million bits per second to the brain for processing, according to *Encyclopedia Britannica,* and yet the conscious mind seems to only process fifty bits per second. Does this mean that all the rest disappears? Absolutely not. The rest is stored subconsciously for times of future access.

If we did not filter all the information received, we would have a problem understanding, prioritizing, and sorting what is useful and

*Influential Rapport*

what is not helpful. We wouldn't get anything done, making for a difficult day. To build a valuable system of information, we learn to sort in incredibly granular ways.

It all comes down to how someone has refined their filters to experience and transmit their experience to others. Consider when a musician is able to perfectly play a piece of music that they have only heard once, or when an experienced builder can tell if a wall is perpendicular. They have refined their filters to transmit their experience. Think about when a chef can tell you exactly what the ingredients are that went into making a delicious meal, or when a great artist can change a painting from something amateur and sloppy to a masterpiece by one stroke of a brush. They, too, have distilled their experience. They are aware, and in their transmission of that awareness, they allow others to experience their knowledge. They are communicating at different levels, and transmitting what they see, feel, hear, taste and smell, leading to profound experiences for others.

When you expand your filters to include becoming aware of others around you, you begin noticing the effect you are having on other people. Because of this, you will have the ability to adjust your communications to your audience. You will become aware of not just the other person's point of view and communication style; you will also be able to decipher the meaning of what that person is saying below the surface level.

Now, you might ask, "what does this mean?" People communicate on several levels at once via verbal and body language and because language contains both ambiguity because we have various words that sound the same (ex.red/read, hi/high etc.) we process the many meanings unconsciously at the speed of thought and apply context to the meaning in order to decipher the meaning of a word in context. Also when we apply body language we add another level of complexity so our ability to gain and maintain others' awareness allows our communication to them to be transmitted smoothly. More importantly, maintaining our awareness of others allows us to decipher their communications to us and allows us to move to the next level of rapport, Attention, when appropriate and desired.

# Chapter 5
# Rapport Level 2 – Attention

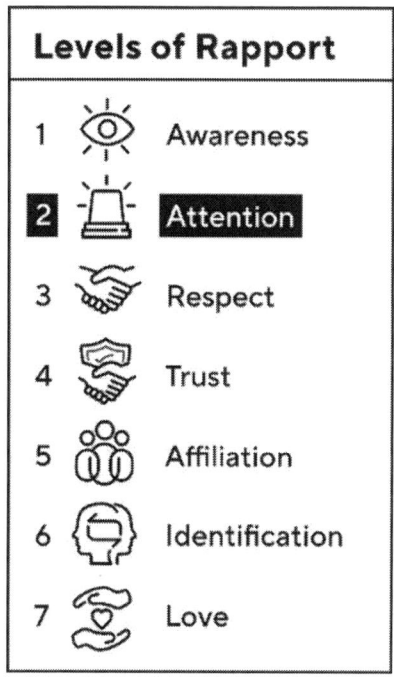

Now that the other person knows and acknowledges that you exist, the next step is to get and keep that person's attention. It is a common trope in movies and television when someone is trying to speak to a desk clerk who's paying attention to the television or a book and listening to another person until something dramatic happens to get the desk clerk's attention. It is even more frustrating in reality when you are interacting on the phone, such as during a customer service call, and you know the other person is giving scripted answers to you rather than listening to what you are saying.

There are times when someone has to be aware that you are speaking with them, and it is the ability to command attention from that standpoint that distinguishes the interaction you will have.

When a magician or stage hypnotist is performing, it is in their performance that they are not only commanding but also directing the audience's attention. The ability to hold a person's attention cuts out other distractions that would otherwise take up perceptual bandwidth.

The ability to direct and misdirect attention is a skill set that can be used in almost every area of your life. Every source of information, every product advertisement, every film, and television show are all vying for your attention, and the more outlandish, garish, and novel, the more likely it is to come into a person's awareness and capture attention.

There's an old saying in the news business, "If it bleeds, it leads." There is supporting evidence throughout the history of journalism that lurid headlines work. The famous New York Post headline "Headless Body Found in Topless Bar," on April 15, 1983, quickly sought attention and even appeared on T-shirts. The phenomenon goes way back to the lurid stories of Jack the Ripper in London in 1888. Phrases evoking fear, curiosity, disgust, and excitement draw on people's natural interest to know more about who, what, why, where, and how behind a story or a trick, ultimately looking for a satisfactory ending to what's being you are presented to them.

We are increasingly inundated with information due to our increased connectivity. We have devices that sit on our desks that bring the world to our attention, devices we wear that give us a constant information feed, handheld devices that buzz, ping and vibrate constantly calling for our attention and because we've been training ourselves to split our attention many different ways, that simple human interaction is often just one of those many calls on our decreasing attention bandwidth.

When we pay attention to another person – now think of the phrase – "pay attention", we're literally spending some of our bandwidth on someone else and we're asking the other person to do the same. Because our attention bandwidth has decreased, like any other commodity it has more value so by literally "paying attention" to someone we're making an offer of adding value to that person which gives us the opportunity to take our rapport level from something strictly transactional to something that has the added value of human interaction which is increasingly being replaced by electronic interaction.

By using the techniques in the later sections of this book, you will learn how to capture and hold attention in a way that directs the other person's thoughts, leading to the next level of rapport.

# Chapter 6
# Rapport Level 3 - Respect

Respect has to be earned. It is an old refrain that respect in this day and age is often demanded but not often earned. Rapport, as a product of earned respect, creates a powerful bond that is difficult to break. Often seen when people don't like each other but work well and effectively together, the respect they build together manifests itself in teamwork and a level of camaraderie that exists outside of liking someone.

There are many examples throughout history of contentious relationships that result in tremendous achievement. Take, for instance, President Truman and General MacArthur. They had a complicated relationship but worked together during the Korean War until that tenuous relationship built only on respect ultimately broke.

The reason for Truman and MacArthur's break is very simple. Rapport built on respect involves setting and maintaining boundaries. When boundaries are violated, there is a sense of injustice and imbalance in the relationship. Therefore, the dynamic exchange of power necessary to maintain rapport is upset where one party feels the other just takes, and they always give. Resentment often builds to the point of passive-aggressiveness and then hostility.

At the same time, rivalries often bring out the best in people, and the respect built on healthy rivalry can motivate people to new heights of performance. This can be best illustrated in sports – primarily because these rivalries are easily visible. Still, if you work in any company, you will see the currents of company politics that inevitably build up in any concentration of people. This is especially true in companies where they tend to focus on hiring "A" players.

These ambitious people typically want to lead and don't want to follow the instructions of others. They often burn out of a company quickly because they don't build rapport based on respect, instead choosing to force compliance either by position or by playing politics. This short term strategy can work but more commonly tends to create more enemies than allies, and over the course of a career, people are inclined to come across each other over and over again. Hence, my advice is to take the longer and more satisfying road of building relationships with vital elements of respect as these will be relationships you will be able to count.

Knowing how to respect boundaries is crucial, especially in our current era, when intentions are often misinterpreted. That is not to say that you can't push boundaries, but you have to know just how far and how fast to go. The feedback from being able to know which level of rapport you are on and how to get to the next one is key in calibrating how to stretch boundaries and with whom.

Another area where the aspect of respect is manifested in rapport is in the area of authority. For example, doctors don't have to wear a lab coat, scrubs, or stethoscope all the time, but they establish authority and, therefore, respect by wearing these symbols of their profession. They expect that people will address them as doctors rather than by their first name, establishing the boundaries of respect and setting the rules for interaction. Other examples are the police officer and their uniform and badge or the use of the title congressman or senator for an elected official. These people are borrowing the respect inherent in the titles and therefore drawing boundaries around the interactions one will have with them.

It is interesting to see what happens when someone breaks these boundaries. The question becomes whether that person is flexible enough to deal with not having the respect that they have come to expect and will be covered in more detail later, and I assure you can be a powerful tool in your influence and persuasion kit.

We gain respect through several means: credentials, fame, wealth, social proof, beauty, athleticism and various kinds of achievement. But it's what we do with this respect that either allows us to build on it to move ot the next level of rapport or if we over-leverage the respect that we have and overstep boundaries which can lead to the loss of respect and the loss of rapport.

How often have we heard about someone who meets a celebrity who treats that person really well? The celebrity, through their status already has a large amount of respect from the general public but in lowering their boundary and acting like a "normal" person the celebrity moves beyond the respect built into status to a respect that is a deeper interpersonal respect which increases rapport.

Unfortunately it's more often the case where the celebrity has a "do you know who I am?" moment that ends up isolating that celebrity from rapport and makes their interactions with the general public transactional.

# Chapter 7
# Rapport Level 4 – Trust

**Levels of Rapport**

1. Awareness
2. Attention
3. Respect
4. **Trust**
5. Affiliation
6. Identification
7. Love

This level of rapport has elements of respect and is very much an extension of respect. After all, how can you ever trust someone who you don't respect? So, how is it different?

You can have respect for someone that you don't trust because respect for skillsets or attributes someone has differs from a personal respect of an individual. I remember seeing Muhammad Ali and Joe Frazier fighting each other in the 'Thrilla in Manila,' their third and final boxing match. It was a brutal fight between two very different men with significantly different worldviews. In the ring, the two were giving their all to knock each other out in a fight that was brutal and

*Influential Rapport*

brilliant. What emerged was much more than a classic boxing event, but because of the brutality of the match, deep respect occurred between the two men.

They never became close friends, but any animosity was put aside, and interactions between them became chiding in nature. They respected each other as fighters and as people. This is something that you see most visibly in sports but also in the world of business where people are vying for mindshare. In business, peers may actually hate each other but often work together when given a common goal if only to make sure their rival doesn't end up getting all the credit for a project. That said, while they have a level of rapport that allows them to work together effectively, especially if they are triangulating animosity towards a third person or group, they likely don't have rapport at the level of trust. Think about it in your own life. Who do you trust? Do you have friends or family with whom you can share anything? Do you segment to whom you reveal things about yourself?

Are there people who just trust anyone? Of course, there are. We all know the story of Jack and the Beanstalk. Jack trades the family cow for magic beans, and his mother is furious about it. Jack has placed his trust in someone whom he really should not have, i.e., moved to a level of rapport that was inappropriate. That Jack ends up breaking into the giant's house, stealing the golden goose, and killing the giant might demonstrate Jack's unworthiness of trust. But that's another story.

Unlike fairy tales, real trust is built on the previous levels of rapport: awareness, attention, and respect. If people are not aware that you exist, they can't trust you, and if you don't know they are there, you can't trust them. If you don't get the other person's attention, that person won't have any experience of what you can and can't do and could have unrealistically high or low expectations of you. Without having that person's attention, you have no way of demonstrating your skills and abilities that lead to respect.

Once you have gained another person's awareness, attention, and respect, the ingredient that further supports trust is consistency. Paraphrasing Bill Buford from his book, *Heat*, the difference between a home cook and a restaurant chef is that ideally, the cuisine a chef prepares should taste the same every time and be exceptional in taste. It is this consistency that distinguishes a great restaurant from a merely good one.

By establishing a consistent pattern of reliability, you can gain the trust of others or lose it irrevocably, depending on the pattern. This consistency creates an expectation in the other person, which is expressed as trust, and these expectations lead to the expansion of any boundaries that were previously set at the respect level. Let's take a closer look at how this happens.

While generally not conscious, there is a risk/reward calculation at play that cannot be overlooked. Risk/reward has beginnings with the origins of our species. In the pure survival situation of early man, what incentive would there have been in sharing resources with anyone outside of one's immediate family? The risk/reward calculation assumes that the person on the receiving end will reciprocate, and when this happens consistently, a basis for trust is established. This is perhaps the most dynamic of the rapport levels because trust has the capability to expand and contract and is sometimes conditional depending on the context.

Consider someone who is consistently on time for work meetings and files their reports on time but repeatedly runs late for family situations. The family learns to tell that person that they are leaving a half-hour earlier than they actually planned, taking into account the consistent tardiness and their trust in this pattern.

Another example of this pattern is someone who is absolutely reliable and does what they say they will do consistently. In work situations, this often leads to promotion and more money with more opportunity to expand boundaries (respect level of rapport) to learn and exhibit skills (attention level of rapport), and to be given greater responsibilities, which lead to greater rewards (trust level of rapport). It is a dynamic process and found across both professional and personal relationships.

In personal relationships, trust is vital. Without it, the boundaries between two people would not allow the exchange of anything beyond a surface connection. While these are generally more than sufficient in work situations, they are hardly a basis for good relationships. It is the expansion of boundaries that lead to friendship, family in the form of a tribe or clan, and the possibility of love, fraternal, or erotic.

Trust is a powerful lever in influence and persuasion. While people have been influenced and persuaded, there is always an element of trust in the equation. Trust often given to someone who has authority in a particular field is a certain level of trust that is transferred to the person based on their authority. When that happens, trust can be fleeting, primarily if expectations are not managed or even set at a wildly different level. This is what a con man does. The effect of that influence is often an enormous backlash against whoever was doing the influencing, and the loss of trust is almost impossible to recover. In the case of someone misusing the trust a person has in a legitimate figure in authority, that trust is often destroyed for a whole class of people, not just the person directly involved. Consider the familiar refrain "You can't trust lawyers" or "How can you tell when a politician is lying? His lips are moving."

In performing in a consistent and positive manner, a person can gain the trust of others, and in that trust, you will be able to leverage the previous rapport levels: awareness, attention, and respect when influencing others. We are persuaded by those we trust. How often have you heard, "You can't trust lawyers, except mine?" The level of rapport built on trust allows you to be the exception to the rules people create in their heads and is the level where relationships transform from being transactional to genuinely relational. It is the level where people move from being customers to clients, and it is the level at which you can create the best or worst of relationships.

# Chapter 8
# Rapport Level 5 - Affiliation

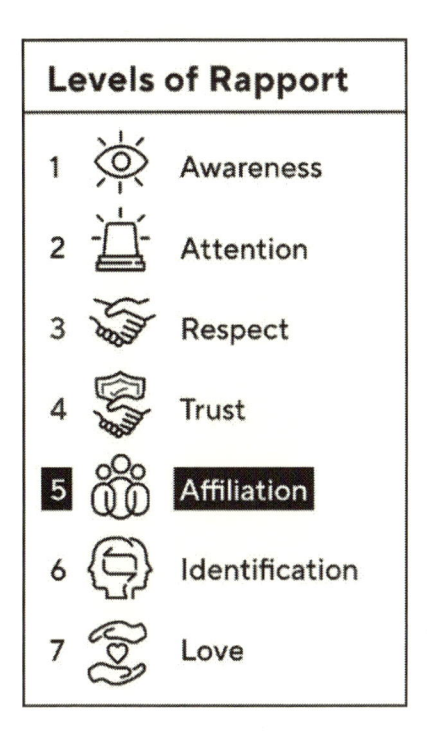

**Levels of Rapport**

| | | |
|---|---|---|
| 1 | 👁 | Awareness |
| 2 | 🚨 | Attention |
| 3 | 🤝 | Respect |
| 4 | 🤝 | Trust |
| **5** | 👥 | **Affiliation** |
| 6 | 🧠 | Identification |
| 7 | 🫶 | Love |

You might be looking at this level and wondering why these are grouped together, primarily because in level four, trust, I outlined some of the weaknesses of authority as a somewhat shallow type of rapport. To a certain extent, that is true. When combined with the other two aspects of affection and admiration, authority is a force multiplier adding both conscious and unconscious push to influence and persuasion done on this level.

After engaging at the trust level and developing that relationship to a high level, the door is open for a deeper and more open exchange of thoughts, plans, aspirations, and engagement.

Because trust allows the stretching of barriers, it can lead to the point of barriers becoming porous, and over time, they can drop altogether in certain contexts. This would be the level of affection and admiration.

I make a distinction here between these two components on this level are based on the amount of reciprocity there is in the rapport. Admiration occurs based more on abilities and skills, with affection being an outcome of how the object of admiration shares or bestows those skills on the admirer. Consider the relationship with a mentor, teacher, or coach. The affection in that relationship is based on what the admired does for the admirer. As an example, it could be how the admirer feels about the interactions or what they get from those interactions, and what they are able to achieve as a result of these interactions.

The admired might be a boss who successfully leads a team and therefore is the person responsible for more wealth in the admirer's life, but the level of interaction is limited by context. There has been a shift in these types of relationships as work culture has become more relaxed over time. Still, because of the more delicate political climate, these boundaries may well become hardened again, and more formal structures may well be put in place. These will be determined by the level of rapport you have with the people you are you are interacting with, and the subsequent techniques will help you navigate these waters.

At this point, it is very important to distinguish between admiration and infatuation or obsession. In rapport, there is always a reciprocal relationship – so at the admiration level, rapport is very much defined by the level of engagement and awareness and acceptance of a mutual relationship. A one-way relationship is not a relationship but rather an imagined representation of a relationship in the mind of the admirer. In short, a fantasy.

*Influential Rapport*

It is really not anything new. It has been the basis of countless romantic comedies where one character becomes infatuated with another character while being unaware of the person to whom they should be drawn. Meanwhile, the object of infatuation, the admired, is unaware of or reacts harshly to the admirer's attempts to gain awareness and attention.

In the real world, this has often become a story of manipulation and exploitation as has been chronicled in the stories of Jeffrey Epstein and NXIVM's Keith Raniere. In this case, the admired ruthlessly used the admirers, and while the admirers thought there was a reciprocal relationship, that rapport only went one way. The paring of admiration and authority created exploitive situations. These are raised not to demonstrate how to create these but to give you the awareness to be able to recognize when it is happening so you will have the knowledge to avoid these situations.

That said, admiration can lead to affinity and affection, so if you think of it as a milestone along the road to rapport, then it becomes a very useful model that allows relationships to deepen immeasurably. Think about it from the standpoint of being the person admired. You are admired for your attributes and abilities, your status, or your accomplishments. Your ideas, once accepted by others create your tribe, which engenders affinity. This is the area of influencers; people follow your thoughts and suggestions based on their admiration for you and the resonance you have created with your opinions and ideas. In this case, it is your attributes and abilities in action that make affinity, and this affinity is the resonance and identification with you. Your admirers want to be like you.

Out of this affinity can come affection, not the type of infatuation that comes from fantasy but a deep appreciation of what the admired has accomplished and has provided for the person who admires. Think of an inspirational leader. They might not know the person in their audience personally but by having the ability to project a caring attitude which could be conveyed in person or via books, video or recordings, or deeds designed to show people how much that person cares, inspires the admirer to identify with the admired. It is in that admiration that affection can result.

The relationship between those involved in motivational seminars as self-help gurus or charismatic celebrities and their audiences differs from a personal, reciprocal relationship. The relationships built between guru or celebrity and audience relate to the form of love known as agape, which is the Greek word generally translated as *spiritual love* and differentiates from more specific forms of love between two people.

When these aspects of the fifth level of rapport come together, they form powerful levers for influence and persuasion. Examples of this include:

Affection | Admiration | Authority | /Affinity

Admiration + Authority = Hierarchical Influence

Admiration + Authority + Affinity = Political Influence

Admiration + Affinity = Social Influence

Affection + Admiration = Celebrity Influence

Affection + Authority = Familial Influence

Affection + Affinity = Tribal Influence

These are the most explicit examples of the blending that can happen with these characteristics at this level. There are other areas of blending that can happen between levels, and as you progress through this book, you will learn more about moving people between levels as you manage your rapport with them.

# Chapter 9
# Rapport Level 6 – Identification

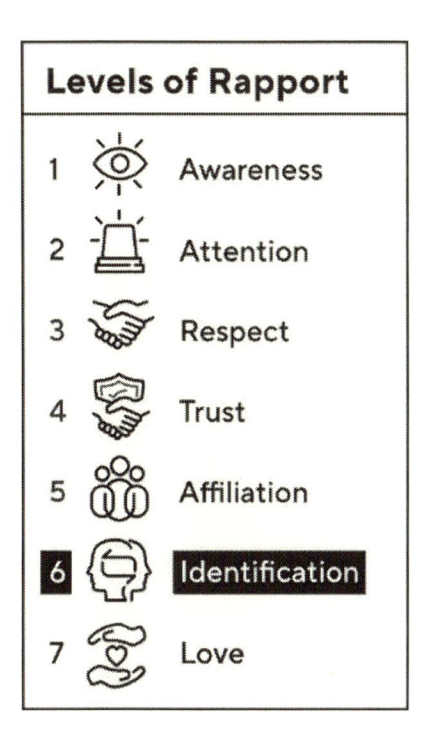

**Levels of Rapport**

1. Awareness
2. Attention
3. Respect
4. Trust
5. Affiliation
6. **Identification**
7. Love

In discussing identification as a rapport level, I am not just discussing physical attraction, although that element certainly does come into play in all human interactions. We are genetically programmed to be drawn to balanced features, body size, and shape as indicators of fertility and good genes.

In this context, I am talking about identification from the standpoint of what you are drawn to, what interests you about a person and what you find attractive in that person. Extending this thought, it is also about what areas in your life are lacking that the other person satisfies. Whether it is companionship, intellectual kinship, political alignment, religious affiliation, or cultural attunement, we look to fill the areas of our lives that are lacking.

This is why people from opposite political viewpoints can be good friends, and people whose religions have been at war with each other for centuries can have a comfortable relationship. Those who might have held only disdain for each other can become close after a shared adventure or hardship. There is a dynamic element of completion and balance that is achieved at the level of attraction. When one person can offer what the other wants, it is very easy to see the level of authority, affiliation, admiration, and affection, but it is when those elements are reciprocated that attraction in rapport occurs.

When these elements come together and are reciprocated, there is a level of intimacy that occurs that can be leveraged in influence and persuasion. It can possibly even be to the detriment of one party. This is illustrated on a broad scale in charismatic leaders who have the ability to lock-in a follower who is already investing that leader with the qualities of authority, affiliation, admiration, and affection and when it is returned to that person by shining a spotlight of reciprocal attraction it can engender fanatical loyalty based on that attraction. Cult leaders, for example, leverage all of these qualities in order to influence and control their followers.

Because there is an inherent power imbalance in this rapport, a slight shift towards equilibrium will be a powerful influence lever on the follower. It is in the recognition which allows that person to borrow a level of authority, affiliation, admiration, and affinity. It confers these traits on that person within the context of a social group.

It is like sitting at the cool kids' table in secondary school, and it is a social dynamic that is present in almost all social groups. Those who choose not to participate, lone wolves, or Sigmas, are seen as weird for not participating. As they get older, because they don't have a need for empowerment within the social dynamic, they are often seen as attractive or charismatic because the lack of need for validation is in itself an attractor.

In influence and persuasion, attraction can be pretty much summed up as "I have what you want, and I am willing to share it if you do what I want you to do." While not a similar situation, it is gentler and more potent than authority, affiliation, admiration, and affection in that there is no element of coercion involved. The person being influenced has concluded that this is what he wants, and so persuasion only involves directing action rather than getting that person to agree to do something.

There is also the phenomenon of *love at first sight*, which is another aspect of attraction. It inspires deep and powerful rapport very quickly between people and often leads to sensory distortion applied to the other person. When it happens, it is often immediate and unexpected, but it is a real phenomenon that is usually random. It is an excellent example of attraction as a level of rapport.

You may be wondering how this is different than the love which I will cover in level seven. The main difference is in the long-term nature of love, which, as the saying goes, "is abiding." Love, at first sight, is a deep rapport that happens unexpectedly. While it can lead to long term love or the seventh level of rapport, it often is passionate, powerful, and short term because it generally lacks the foundations of love and, in many ways, shares the characteristics of infatuation. Fragile in many ways, it is extremely enticing, exciting and passionate, and in many ways, it is all the things that our society tells us romantic love should be.

I remember the first time I fell in love at first sight. I was in secondary school. One day, I had a chance to speak with an individual whom I'd never spoken to before, and suddenly it was like looking down a tunnel where her face was the only thing in focus. All my awareness was tuned in on her, and I could tell that it was the same with her. We were in deep rapport, which seemed to come out of nowhere. Of course, I now know there is a process to it, but at the time, it was new, exciting and very soon became passionate. After a couple of weeks, however, we found out we didn't have a foundation for a rapport based on love, but for those few weeks, it sure felt like we did, and just as quickly as it started, it stopped.

Attraction as a tool of influence and persuasion can be enticing and powerful when someone understands how to maintain that attraction by balancing authority, affiliation, admiration, and affection. They can leverage those characteristics into a system that can sustain itself with little maintenance.

# Chapter 10
# Rapport Level 7 – Love

**Levels of Rapport**

1. Awareness
2. Attention
3. Respect
4. Trust
5. Affiliation
6. Identification
7. **Love**

Love is the most powerful and most long-lasting level of rapport. It encompasses all the previous levels while adding its own unique properties to the mix. Unlike attraction, which is more like a sprint, love is a marathon. This level of rapport covers love between two adults, love of a parent and a child, love for family and friends, and love for a pet.

One of the critical distinctions in this model is the type of boundaries that are inherent in the levels.

## Influential Rapport Boundaries

| Level of Rapport | Boundaries and Strength |
|---|---|
| Awareness | Strong - meant to protect the individual |
| Attention | Strong - but more flexible due to engagement with another person |
| Respect | Firm - to describe the nature of interaction for both parties and equality within an interaction |
| Trust | Elastic - due to the successful repetition of interaction allowing for greater flexibility of action |
| Affiliation - Affection/Admiration/Affinity | Flexible - within a dynamic ecosystem usually working to find a balance between participants |
| Identification | Stretchable - dependent on the dynamics of Rapport continuing to satisfy participants but can lead to a hardening of boundaries should Rapport slip out of this level |
| Love | Loose - allowing for the greatest flexibility of action |

With love, unlike the other levels, there is little ongoing attention to boundaries unless one is blatantly crossed. But even then, there is more leeway in how the individuals handle the situation because rapport is solid at this level, and both sides are invested in the relationship. In comparison, at the attraction level, one boundary crossed can lead to an analysis of everything in that relationship that is not ideal, which can be magnified in the imagination of the person whose Boundary was violated.

*Influential Rapport*

At the love level, the individuals involved are much more likely to ignore smaller transgressions and work out differences. Because they have invested in every previous step of the rapport bond, it is based on more things than passion and momentum.

It is this deep investment in the rapport bond that overshadows any boundary, and something catastrophic has to happen for that bond to be destroyed. Consider cheating on a partner. If you have been cheated on before, and this is the one boundary that you have drawn that a partner should not cross, this could be the one area that would break that rapport. The deeper investment in the relationship, the more difficult the break would be to repair.

In the area of influence, love will overcome almost any other emotion. We will do nearly anything for those we love and will go above and beyond where we thought our boundaries lie. The obvious example is what a mother will sacrifice for her child. There are countless examples of mothers giving up their lives for their children – even those children still in the womb.

Other examples of this exist outside of the mother-child bond, and it is in the understanding of this level that influence and persuasion will be the most potent mechanism. Because people will do anything for those they love, when you lead someone to believe what they are doing will benefit their loved ones or keep those loved ones from harm, they will conclude that any act is justified. This type of leverage is often used in propaganda and is exceptionally useful in moving people from one point of view to another.

In their push for power, Communists all over the world appealed to the proletariat. Yes, they were talking about fairness and exploitation, etc. but it all came down to the essential message, "Don't you want to give your children a better life?" The promise of a better life helped to perpetuate a system that could not deliver that better life because it was built on a faulty premise. The increasingly connected world allowed people to see how the rest of the world lived – the better life was outside of the Communist bloc and so quite literally, the walls came down, and the impetus to give the children they loved a better life helped end the Cold War.

I have made a very successful career as an executive recruiter, and part of the job is placing people in high-level positions within companies. I have always prided myself on doing what is best for the candidate I am recruiting while taking care of the corporate, or hiring, client. While these two impulses might seem opposed, they are aligned to the point of being two sides of the same coin.

The quicker you fill a position, the better it is as it leads to more work from that client. A candidate that I had been working with for a while was a great fit for a new position. He checked all the boxes that the corporate hiring client had listed and was even willing to move himself and his family across the country for the job. The candidate told me that even though he would be leaving his parents and extended family, he had to take this opportunity for his wife and children. For him, this was his ultimate way of caring for his family. He would be making a lot more money; they would be able to afford a much better lifestyle, and there was only an upside from the professional and financial aspects of the company he would join. It seemed like a no-brainer in applying for and accepting this position.

We were getting very close to the interview stage with the corporate hiring company, which I was certain he would ace. He seemed to be the right person for the job. So while I was preparing him for moving to the next stage, I asked him if he had discussed relocation with his family. He hadn't.

He told me that he was sure that the family would relocate because this new location was very desirable, and they would have a much better lifestyle. Although I was taking the chance on losing the best candidate that I had for the particularly difficult search, I urged him to have a sincere, heart to heart conversation with his wife and children before deciding to move forward.

I understood that he was expressing his love for his wife and children by sacrificing his time with his aging parents and extended family. When he discussed this opportunity with them as a real possibility, it turned out that this was not a move that they supported. His attempt to show his love for his family blinded him to what they actually wanted – they loved being near his parents and having their cousins in their lives.

They say love is blind, but it is more like love can be blinding, and because of that deep level of rapport, as a tool of influence and persuasion, it has the ability to co-opt motives, strategies, and values. The skill of being able to step out of the love haze in any situation allows you to actively assess if you are making the right decisions based on hard reality rather than the haze of hope that love tends to exude. In your personal interactions, you will be able to better understand and predict the decisions of others when they are in rapport at the love level.

# Part 2

# Chapter 11
# How to Gain Rapport

**Drew's Story**

When I was in secondary school, I knew a guy named Drew. He was pretty ordinary and fit in well but was neither the most popular kid nor the least popular. Drew had the opportunity to become an exchange student for our sophomore year, and when he came back, it was like he was a different person. His manner, the way he moved through the world, was different, and he suddenly had the ability to interact with people very differently than he had before.

He wasn't suddenly European, but looking back on it, he did learn to connect with people differently than he had before. We had an opportunity to discuss it back then, and what follows are some tips that he gave me based on his experience of being transplanted to a foreign country for a year.

- He made an effort to learn the culture.
- Although people there, for the most part, spoke English, he made an effort to learn their language.
- He didn't hide the fact that he was American.
- He took particular notice of how people acted in certain situations.
- He looked for things to appreciate about the culture.
- He made an effort to stay in touch with the people with whom he had created relationships.

Thinking back on it, he hit every level of the rapport process.

## Awareness

As a teenager, landing in a foreign country and staying with a host family can be both exhilarating as well as frightening. Even though Dutch culture is similar to American – mostly due to American military presence and even more so because of the influence of American entertainment on television, it is a distinct culture with a proud history. As cosmopolitan a society as it is, being aware of the social norms of any society will allow you to move within that society even as a stranger, and the Netherlands is no exception.

The famous coffee shops are places where you can buy and smoke marijuana openly as it is commonly accepted, but trying to buy and use hard drugs is very much frowned upon.

To his credit, Drew took the opportunity to observe and notice the differences between American and Dutch cultures and, rather than just focusing on the differences, he focused on what they had in common. You would think that "fitting in" would make him disappear in the crowd, but because of his awareness of his surroundings, he stood out because of the typical stereotype of the loud American tourist with which everyone is familiar.

In any situation, people will have a pre-conceived idea about you based on the way you look, the way you dress, the way you speak, and the way you act. This could be right but is often wrong. When you are aware of the image you are projecting, you can leverage that by playing it up or by destroying their idea by acting against expectations.

If everyone expects you to be the loud American tourist, in the right situation it could be a useful strategy to exaggerate it to the point of comedy. When you stop the act, the contrast will be even more effective than the stereotype. This is a strategy that requires a great deal of both situational awareness and sensory acuity to be able to gauge the reaction of the people with whom you are interacting. But when done right, the contrast can destroy the picture they have of the loud American tourist, and they are left with the person you are presenting to them.

The second strategy Drew used was to blend in, but when they would speak with him, they quickly learned that he was an American, and they were surprised and happy with the way he acted because of the stereotype they had held in their mind about Americans.

## Application

### Awareness Exercise

The key element for developing awareness is developing your sensory acuity, or in other words, being able to shift the filters that you use to get by in everyday life and let yourself process information purposefully. We develop filters to avoid sensory overload and to make sense of our environment. We are generally aware enough to avoid walking into other people in a crowded mall, and we laugh when someone is so distracted that they walk into something like a parking meter.

Our minds are built for taking in sensory input and then filtering what we need in order to survive, and in taking control of these filters, you will allow yourself to become more aware of other people around you and the effect you are having on them. It will also allow you to gain their awareness because, like you were before you began doing this exercise, their filters aren't fine-tuned.

This is an exercise that you can do by yourself and does not require a partner. A partner version of this exercise can be found in my book *The 5 Keys To Hypnotic Selling*, but I have found in working with my coaching clients that it is best to take advantage of the environment around you. While being able to work with a partner can give great results, it is better to get started as soon as possible in

*Influential Rapport*

developing your skills. This exercise can be used in any public situation where people are not rushing around, so if you are in a restaurant or a mall where people are sitting or standing but not rushing around you will.

Part 1

1. Find a place where you can observe another person. It could be in a mall where you will likely find sitting areas for people either taking a rest or waiting for someone.
2. Set yourself off to the side or preferably opposite someone whom you can discretely observe.
3. Take a moment to center yourself, taking a deep breath and closing your eyes, relax and understand that you are simply going to observe the other person.
4. Open your eyes and soften your focus. Using your peripheral vision and, without any judgment, take a quick look at the other person. Notice how that person is sitting, their arm position, head position, the position of their feet. Do this for a count of two.
5. Close your eyes for a count of two and then open them again. Using your peripheral vision again, quickly notice any changes in the person's posture or position. If there is no change, close your eyes for another count of two and open your eyes, noticing if there's any change in the person you are observing.
6. Note any changes and move on to someone else and repeat the process.

Part 2

In this part of the exercise, I am going to add another element that will help you open your filters and activate both your conscious and unconscious mind so you may become more aware.

1. Repeat steps one through four from above and this time:

2. Match your body posture to the person you are observing. You don't have to be perfect; just approximate the other person's position. After you have got the position, close your eyes for a count of two.
3. Open your eyes and notice any changes in the posture of the person you are observing, and if you feel like shifting, let yourself also shift because your unconscious is picking up on things more quickly than your conscious mind.
4. Notice how close you have come to approximating the pose of the person you are observing.

After you have done both exercises a few times with one person, find another person to do this with and repeat the exercises. I would suggest you do it a several times with different people and then let it drop for a while. Then go back to it, and it will soon become very easy for you just to move to match what you observe without having to process the information.

People are more comfortable with sameness than differences because, on the unconscious level, differences can be interpreted as dangerous, and sameness has a genuine level of familiarity. This skill, referred to as *matching and mirroring,* has many uses in gaining rapport that I will go into later in the book. The skill will allow you to begin to open interactions easily and help remove resistance to moving to the next rapport level.

Attention

First, it is important to remember that you can't gain rapport with someone when you don't know that person exists, and it is even more challenging when that person doesn't know you exist. Second, without awareness of how your interaction is affecting the other person, you will not know if it is a passing interest or something more, or if what you are saying or doing is causing the other person to want to run away screaming. Not paying attention could cause something far worse than unawareness to happen. It could cause a person to fight off any attempt to actively build rapport.

Drew, my high school friend who went abroad as an exchange student, was able to pay attention and give attention. He made sure that he was picking up on the local customs and way of life, and those attempts were what turned Americanisms from mistakes to endearing if somewhat quirky habits. By paying attention, he was able to recognize patterns of boundaries that made social interactions possible. In every culture, these patterns are classified as polite or civil behavior. Things that operate outside of these patterns are viewed as rude, or worse, anti-social. It is in knowing where these boundaries are that allows a stranger to function in society and, at times, stretch these boundaries without alienating oneself.

As a culture, the Dutch are known for being blunt, for lack of a better word. For those who aren't used to this style of communication, it can seem cold, off-putting, and, to a certain extent, hostile. For the Dutch, the directness is a matter of honesty and efficiency and a sign that a person is not trying to influence with pretty words. Directness is prized, and not being direct could be taken for an indication of dishonesty.

Drew said that at first, he was surprised by how direct the Dutch people were. My friend Drew, and I are New York City natives, and we are often thought of as being blunt to the point of rudeness. But in our opinions, Dutch are far more direct. By directing his attention to the intention behind the communication rather than just the words, Drew came to understand that the Dutch people weren't rude; they had a style of communication that was slightly different than what he was used to. In adapting to that style of communication, he was able to build relationships that moved beyond the surface.

In doing this, he was not only able to gain their attention but also keep their attention. Communicating in the style of the person you are communicating with allows for the easy transmission of information. It is the difference between having to translate from another language to yours and easily being able to concentrate on the message, and the delivery is not distracting from the contents.

There's something compelling about giving someone your attention. When you do that, it is like shining a spotlight on a person and acknowledging that person exists. In this day and age, many people feel that they are getting lost in the crowd, and this can account for people seeking attention on social media. They are not getting much of its satisfactory attention in their interpersonal relationships. They are seeking attention, and when you give it, they respond in kind, and that is where the next step from awareness opens into an opportunity for deeper rapport.

By now, I trust you have had the opportunity to play with the awareness exercises because experience with those will help you get better, faster as we move into more complex skill sets. A structure always has a strong foundation, and it is in these essential skill sets that you are developing that are building your foundation to use additional skills masterfully.

As illustrated in Drew's story, the ability to adapt your communications to the style of the person you are communicating with is a powerful way to get and keep someone's attention. While it is easy to get attention, if you are speaking in jargon or with a heavy foreign accent different from the listener's, keeping that attention will be another hurdle to overcome. When communications are delivered in a way that is not jarring to the senses, the delivery smooths the way for your message to be accepted.

The next exercise will help you enhance your sensitivity to how people around you are speaking, and by adopting that mode of speech, you will be able to create and maintain rapport with that person much

*Influential Rapport*

better. You can play with this skill set in any interaction where you will be talking with another person.

Attention Exercise #1

Decide that you are going to play with this exercise, and while you are doing that, you will put aside the previous exercise. At this point, one of the things that hold people back is trying to do too much at one time. After a while, you will be able to blend the skill sets, but at this point, getting comfortable with each skill set discretely will allow you to make progress more quickly. When you do this, you will soon find them integrating naturally in your everyday interactions.

1. Set your intention to perform the exercise while interacting with other people in your life, whether it is those you see and speak with daily or just someone you are talking to in passing.
2. When you speak with that person, notice how quickly or slowly that person is saying and when it is your turn, talk to that person at the same speed. At this point, the content will be based on what your conversation is supposed to be about. The main thing to play with in this exercise is to match the speed at which the other person is speaking.
3. At first, if the person is speaking very fast or very slow, it might seem to be challenging to keep your thoughts together. That is why I suggest you save this exercise for when you are in a transactional situation or something that is not a serious conversation. When you get better at this, you will be able to use it in very high-pressure situations to significant effect.
4. Notice the effect that changing the speed of your speech to the other person's has on that person. He or she will likely not have a huge reaction, but you will probably notice a deepening of breath, a relaxing of the shoulders, and more smiles as you are speaking.
5.

## Attention Exercise #2

Now that you have successfully been able to match the other person's talking speed, notice that they are taking in your messages at a deeper level and responding with more interest or at least, not rejecting your message outright. With your attention tuned to the other person and while you are noticing the impact of your communications, it is time to develop the next level, which will be an extension of the previous exercise.

1. Decide that you are going to play with this exercise, and while you are doing that, you will put aside the previous activity. After a while, you will be able to blend the skill sets, but at this point, get comfortable with each skill set discretely. When you do this, you will soon find them integrating naturally in your everyday interactions.
2. Like before, perform this while speaking with people you meet in everyday life. You can, of course, find a partner to do this, but it is not necessary, and a partner might be around a lot, but there are people all around you that you can use to hone your skills while at the same time making your communications with them better and more comfortable which will give better rapport with them.
3. When you speak with that person, notice the types of words they are using to describe events. What kinds of words is that person using to describe sensory experiences? Examples include:

    a. Visual (Visual references)
        i. Bright
        ii. Shiny
        iii. Dark

b. Auditory (Audio references)
   i. Loud
   ii. Muffled
   iii. Discordant

c. Kinesthetic (Feeling references)
   i. Hard
   ii. Soft
   iii. Mushy

d. Olfactory (Sense of smell references)
   i. Stinks on ice
   ii. The smell of Victory
   iii. Stink of failure

e. Gustatory (Sense of taste references)
   i. The sweet taste of victory
   ii. Leaves a sour taste in my mouth
   iii. That's a spicy story

At first, just concentrate on noticing one of these categories. To begin with, notice visual words since they are more prevalent in our language and used in more situations. Then after you have started noticing visual words, and are comfortable knowing how a person is expressing themselves, move to filtering for auditory words.

Chances are by the time you have finished filtering for visual words, you will have already begun to notice the auditory and kinesthetic words people are using. Keep doing this until you are comfortable that you are catching these types of words when someone is using them. At this point, you can feel free to do this without a partner, and if you are somewhere in public, like the place where you were practicing your awareness exercises, you can listen to conversations other people are having and filter the kinds of words they are using as well. The point is not to eavesdrop on their conversation, as most peoples' conversations are not that interesting, but begin to open up your filters and pay attention to the kinds of words people are using.

Attention Exercise #3

This is an extension of the previous exercise. Before you were concentrating on noticing what kinds of words – visual, auditory, kinesthetic, olfactory, gustatory (VAKOG) – people are using. And as good as that exercise is for building your competence to pay attention, it doesn't include reciprocal interaction. Now that you are comfortable listening, it is time to start speaking and creating rapport through your enhanced ability to pay attention.

1. Remember to set your intention to concentrate on this exercise while you are doing it and hold back on adding things from the other exercises at this time. Everything will start to come together naturally once you are comfortable with each exercise.
2. While interacting and speaking with people, notice the types of words they are using (VAKOG).
3. Now that you notice the types of words they are using begin employing their words. For example, someone says, "I would like to buy some **big red roses**." You could say, "Great, I have some **big red roses**, right here," as opposed to saying, "I'll show you some roses." By using their words at this stage, you put yourself in the position of communicating rather than analyzing what they are saying, matching it up against the chart of VAKOG words, previously shown and trying to have a regular interaction – all at the same time.
4. Be aware of the effect that you are having and pay attention to the other person's reactions. This is where it pays to say less and listen more. They will give you other keywords when they speak because they are describing their experience of the world, their interaction with you, what they want, or how, they

are in essence, telling you how they want you to communicate with them.
5. Hold off on repeating everything the other person says. Pick only a few words that seem to have significance to them. It could be how they emphasize that word when they say it; it could be a pause before saying a word. After practicing this exercise, you will be able to pick these up quickly.
6. Notice if the other person relaxes when speaking with you and how the conversation flows because when you are comfortable with this, your conversations will naturally become smoother and easier because you are speaking the same language.

These are the beginning stages of this skillset, and these exercises are designed to make it easier to begin communicating at the awareness and attention Levels in order to build and maintain rapport. More advanced versions of these exercises are available online at: www.influentialrapport.com.

# Chapter 12

# Leveraging Rapport

### Level 3 – Respect

| # | Levels of Rapport |
|---|---|
| 1 | Awareness |
| 2 | Attention |
| **3** | **Respect** |
| 4 | Trust |
| 5 | Affiliation |
| 6 | Identification |
| 7 | Love |

Respect is the third level of rapport, and and in order to understand it, it's important to first identify where your own boundaries are so you can set what is negotiable and what is not. Discovering the limits, or boundaries, of others, but not knowing your own first keeps you at the level of being a cog in a machine or a tool in another's hands rather than making yourself a valued partner in the interaction.

Knowing your boundaries will also allow you to make sure that you maintain your own code of conduct. While I am not going to tell you when to use the influence and persuasion skills you are learning in this book, I suggest that it is always best, to be honest, and straightforward with people. Do what you say you are going to do and treat people well. People with whom you form deep rapport connections are lowering their boundaries for you, and any kind of betrayal of these boundaries will hurt your reputation and, at worse, make you an enemy.

**Drew's Story**

When Drew was on his student exchange trip to the Netherlands, he was interested in making new friends and having a great experience. He was smart and friendly, which naturally goes over well in any environment, and he was keenly aware that he was not in New York City and therefore paid attention to the style of communication and the customs of the Netherlands. There was one thing about Drew that stood out in the Netherlands. Drew is not a minority. With light brown/blond hair and blue eyes, he did not stand out in that way. The Netherlands is a country known for having the tallest average population in the world. At five foot four, Drew is short. In the Netherlands, five foot four is not just short for a man; it is short for anyone.

Commonly, for secondary schoolboys, there is typically competition for a place, even dominance, in the social hierarchy. It did not matter that Drew was only going to be in the Netherlands for one year, for the time he was there, he would have to carve out his place in that social hierarchy and set boundaries within the broader social context of the school.

Although known as a socially tolerant country, this was still secondary school, and secondary schools are the same everywhere in the world in terms of social hierarchies amongst the students. You have your cool kids, your jocks, your nerds, your musicians, and you have the group that doesn't fit in with everyone else. In this context, how would Drew navigate the hierarchical maze?

Although short, Drew had joined the secondary school's wrestling team as a freshman. He was in great shape, and due to the confidence he had built as a competitive wrestler, he was able to draw on that confidence and brush off any attempt by the taller kids attempting to intimidate him. He marked a boundary. While there were areas where he would naturally give in, learning to fit in, Drew marked his boundaries about how far he was willing to go in situations and where he would draw the line.

One example was with girls. When he asked out a popular girl who happened to be several inches taller than him, she told him that she couldn't go out with him because he was shorter than her, and she thought they wouldn't look right together. Drew answered, "That just means that you could, you are just not. Because if you are worried about what other people think rather than how good a time we would have together, then we shouldn't go out. After all, if what your friends think is more important than what you feel, then we're not right for each other." Calling out this boundary that she had, caused her to examine it. Had she really thought about it?

She changed her mind, and while they didn't have a long-lasting romance, they remained friends after that because he realized that her boundary was built on what she thought other people would think. By holding on to his own boundaries and bringing her attention to hers, he persuaded her to realize that her boundary wasn't immutable when seen from a different perspective.

Notice, he did not insult her or violate her boundaries; he merely asked her to reexamine them in context and tested them while still respecting them. Not reacting to what she said initially as an insult, Drew was commanding respect rather than demanding it.

For the other teens fighting over the pecking order, Drew had a choice, try to be the alpha of the group, take a subordinate beta position or not participate. Again, he marked his boundaries, in this case leveraging his status as an outsider, becoming neutral in the political games commanding respect from the various groups by being open and friendly but not joining any. Because of that, he was able to circulate multiple cliques while maintaining rapport. While not necessarily included in any of the cliques, Drew wasn't explicitly excluded from them.

**Application**

Exercise #1– Finding Your Boundaries

To command respect, you have to be able to draw boundaries, and this exercise is the first step.

1. Get a pen and some paper. You can use a ballpoint, a fountain pen, a Sharpie, a marker, it doesn't matter, but you want something with a certain amount of permanence. Writing it on your phone or a computer doesn't have the same tactile feel that you will get from writing it down, and it is this feeling that will help encode in your mind what you are writing.
2. Pick a situation you want to draw a boundary around; it could be how you want to be treated by a boyfriend or girlfriend; it could be how you want to be treated by your boss. Whatever the situation, there will be boundaries that you want but likely have never expressed even if only to yourself.
3. At the top of the first page, write: "What's important to me about [fill in the situation you are using for the exercise]."
4. Write down five key things that are important to you – it could be more if you come up with more, but target at least five. Do this quickly and put down whatever first comes to mind because you want your most honest and non-judged answers here.
5. Read through them and notice if anything is missing that should be there. This is for you, and no one else will be reading this unless you want that person to, so feel free to be as honest

as you can because otherwise, the only person you are fooling is yourself.
6. Read through the list, and once you have, number them in order of importance with number one being the most important, two the second most important, and so on.
7. Once they have been numbered, look at them again, and on another sheet of paper, start writing down which one, or perhaps more, you can do without and consider how removing it, or them, changes your perception of the other ones. You might notice as some do, that several of these are very similar and can be combined into something much more substantial that fits better on your list
8. Now that you have your list, which ones on the list are items that you will absolutely not tolerate someone crossing. Not to say, you have to break relations with someone who does, but clarify which behaviors you will and will not put up with by others.
9. Repeat this for every situation you will want to draw boundaries around, and soon you will find a common theme running between them. Once you have completed the next exercise, you will further develop those attributes necessary for commanding respect.

Exercise #2 – Consequences of Boundary Violations

1. You have your list created in the previuos exercise. Now on another page, write down at the top: "What I am willing to do to defend my boundaries" because you have to clarify in your own mind what your course of action will be if someone violates your boundaries. Failing to do so is a failure to command respect. Target at least five options for yourself.
2. You have a wide array of options for consequences of boundary violations. Some ideas include breaking off contact, having a heart to heart talk, escalating the situation to someone

of greater authority, etc. Having the options clarified and laid out now will help you determine what and how you will realistically control how you are treated and how you will command respect.
3. Once you have added your options, have another look at your list and be honest with yourself regarding whether these are things that you are absolutely willing to do and if not, then write down notes for yourself under a new title: "What I have to learn or develop so I can respond the way I want to."

Exercise #3 – Developing Boundaries for Self

This exercise begins precisely the same way as the others except for what you will write at the top of a new page.

1. At the start of a new page, draw a line down the middle of the page, top to bottom.
2. On the left side, write: "Boundaries for Myself," this is for behaviors that you will not tolerate for yourself. If you can't hold yourself to standards to the point where you can respect yourself, how can you expect others to give you respect? Target at least five boundaries that you won't tolerate in yourself. You can put down more but target at least five.
3. At the top right side of the page, write: "How I will act instead." Write down how you will act, stating them in the positive. For example, rather than writing, "I won't let myself overeat," you will reframe it and write, "I will make sure to eat healthy to stay fit."
4. Make these lists for each situation where you want to draw boundaries for yourself.

| Boundaries for Myself | How I Will Act Instead |
|---|---|
| Sleeping half the day away | Getting up when the alarm clock goes on at 8:00 am |
| Snacking on potato chips and cookies | Drink a glass of water or eat a piece of fruit |
| Visiting that toxic family member which always puts me in a foul mood | Visiting someone else who I enjoy |

There will certain situations that you should not put up with, and preparing for these will alleviate the fight or flight response that often happens when we feel that we are not getting the respect that we deserve. When our boundaries are violated this type of preparation will provide a more thought out range of appropriate responses than those that come as a reaction to stress.

These are the first steps in establishing your own boundaries and therefore being more competent in commanding respect. The exercises will involve learning where the boundaries of others lie because they won't tell you, not because they don't want you to know but because they haven't crystalized them in their own mind. How often have you had a partner who is upset because you did or didn't do something that they thought was important? You had no clue you were crossing a boundary and causing your partner to feel disrespected because that partner had not made that boundary clear. Many of these boundaries are things that we learned as children as typical aspects of our family dynamics. The disconnect is in understanding that the way that your family operated and the expectations developed in that dynamic differ between families. This was demonstrated in Drew's story.

The next step is learning how to determine what other peoples' boundaries are because to command respect, you have first to give respect. Just as Drew gave respect by observing the boundaries in the society around him and within the new school he was attending, your first step is being aware that such boundaries exist. In every culture, there is a certain amount of acceptable personal space that a person is expected to maintain, at least until you have gotten past the respect stage of rapport.

In the US, this distance is between two to three feet or sixty to ninety centimeters. One study says that Romanians are comfortable with four-and-half feet or 140.2 cm. This, of course, changes when the rapport becomes more profound at the trust level and beyond.

Respect Exercise #4 – Finding Others' Boundaries

1. As with the other exercise in this book, the first step to finding others' boundaries is to know they exist. Go out into a public place and notice the distance that people maintain. Are they close together or not? Do they hold a certain amount of distance, or is it flexible?
2. Notice through the distance that people have represents the level of rapport they have with each other. If they maintain a social space of three feet or more, then they do not have a strong rapport and are likely in the awareness and attention levels.
3. Notice the orientation of their bodies. Are they facing each other? If so, they are likely building their rapport and are moving toward the respect level. If they are partially turned away as if they are going to walk away, then they haven't yet built the basis for moving to the respect level and are still feeling each other out. Pay particular attention to the lower body as that is an unconscious indication that the other person is ready to move on either about their business or just away from the person to whom they are talking.
4. If they are closer than three feet and are at approximately two feet difference, then they have likely moved to the respect

stage. At this stage, their bodies are more likely oriented towards each other, and they are more likely tuning everyone else out.
5. Once you begin noticing the unconscious levels of rapport that people are broadcasting, that will allow you to understand the level of rapport the person you are interacting with will be comfortable with before trying to move on to another too soon.
6. The next step will be to begin adding in the skills you have gained in previous exercises.

Respect Exercise #5 – Finding Others' Boundaries

This process is very similar to discovering your own boundaries, and the process builds great rapport when you do it well. The critical thing to remember here is that when asking the question, it is essential to be genuinely curious; otherwise, it can seem like an interrogation, and you would get the opposite of what you are trying to do.

1. Become genuinely curious. Are you curious about something, or have you been curious about something in the past? Remember that time and notice how you feel now about it or felt at the time, and when you have it, make sure that you can recall it either by the way it feels, how you look at something, or what you say to yourself.
2. Soften your question to the other person by prefacing your question with: "I am curious..." or "I was wondering..."
3. Ask the other person, "What's important to you about (whatever you want to know about that person's boundaries in that situation)." Example: "I was wondering, what's important to you about (situation)?"
4. You have the option of following the question up immediately, or if the person asks why you want to know, you might

consider answering: "Because I want to know how we can best work together on this." Example: "I was wondering, what's important to you about (situation) because I just want to know how we can best work together on this." When you ask this way, you will usually get a much more in-depth answer than in a mundane interaction, and you will be building rapport while you are doing this because you are respecting the other person's boundaries.

# Chapter 13

# Trust

Most transactional business situations will generally be confined to the first three levels of rapport: awareness, attention, and respect. In order to truly have rapport at these levels, they have to work together. When you have respect, you are drawing awareness and attention to yourself, which will allow you to provide proof of reciprocating the respect rapport bond. That said, it is also an opportunity to break that bond because there are expectations inherent in the relationship, i.e., that you will do what you say you will do, and so will the other person. This is why you can have respect for someone who demonstrates good skills, but that respect will only extend to the skills, not to the person, and if there is any relationship at all there, it will be too transactional with the emphasis on boundaries in the form of contracts.

Repeated demonstrations of respect for boundaries at the respect level will take the relationship to the next level, which is trust. By repeatedly conforming to the boundaries set at the respect level, those boundaries start to become more porous, and more leeway is given between the participants.

Trust Exercise #1 – Building Trust

As stated before, Trust is built over repeated demonstrations of respect. This process can be accelerated by leveraging the other levels of rapport in order to create a trust bond exceptionally quickly.

Make sure you are comfortable with the skills you have developed with the previous exercises. Work on them until you notice that you have a fundamental level of competency that you are verifying

*Influential Rapport*

in everyday life. It is worth taking the time because the skills that you are going to be developing moving forward will not have the same impact without the ones from the previous levels. If you are not comfortable keeping and maintaining awareness, attention, and respect, while you may gain trust, it will be tough keeping it.

1. Use the skills you have developed to gain awareness, attention, and respect. When you are on the respect level, learn the other person's boundaries.
2. As an extension of the previous exercise, this time, you will use your knowledge of their boundaries to deepen your rapport. The act of eliciting those boundaries will get you to the trust level very quickly, and this is also where you are going to begin combining skills. Because you have been paying close attention and have opened your awareness, you will hear that in describing their boundaries, there will be one that the person will be emphasizing. This will be the one that is most important and can include the following:

    a. The person will take a deep breath before expressing that particular boundary
    b. The person will pause, and there will be a slight shift in the person's voice as they emphasize that boundary
    c. There will be slight flushing of the skin when that person talks about the boundary

3. By opening up your senses through the previous exercises, you will soon be picking these cues up automatically, and when you do, that is the area you will be exploring in more detail.

4. Using the same process, you can ask, "Just so I understand you, what's important about (the boundary that person just expressed)" and take note of what things are inside that boundary.

a. Another way to ask this question is, "Just so I understand you, what does (the boundary the person expressed) mean for you?"

5. This process, just by bringing a person through it, will foster tremendous Rapport and move you to the beginning of the trust level.

Because people are rarely, if ever asked these questions, they are not prepared for them and do not have their boundaries set against them. You are essentially moving around the boundaries, and this will allow you to use this knowledge to deepen the rapport at the trust level.

Trust Exercise #2

One of the essential things about being someone that is trusted is that there is a dynamic exchange of ideas, interests, goals, and solutions. So now that you know what is essential for the other person, to continue to build trust, you have to come forward with solutions. Ultimately, without solutions, you are an order taker, and while you may be respected for your abilities and have a low level of trust to carry out tasks, you can never be in an equal, partnership type of relationship.

This partner relationship is not only relegated to the work environment. For two people to have a true partnership, the relationship best works when there is a reciprocal exchange – even if one seemingly dominates the other. That is the role the other person will not only be accepting but embracing for the relationship to work out.

1. By now, you have been able to elicit the other person's boundaries, make a note of the especially important one and go more deeply into them with the person, i.e., "What's

important about (the particular boundary that person emphasized)" or "What does (boundary) mean for you?"
2. Talk about what you are doing together or the solution you have for that person using the boundaries that the person mentioned to you. Example: If one of the critical boundaries is being on time, or as some people say, "I don't like to be kept waiting," as you are talking about doing something with that person, you could mention, "And I hate being kept waiting so I'll make sure you aren't either."
3. Continue to use their own words. This is similar to the earlier exercise, *Attention Exercise #3*, except that not only are you using the same type of words the other person is using, but you are also using the same boundaries. You have re-drawn the boundaries to include you.
4. Follow through on what you say you are going to do. Once you have gained respect and built trust, nothing destroys it faster than violating that trust.

It is important to remember that without all of the previous levels, you can't build a positive rapport at the trust level and above. You can, however, create a negative rapport at that level easily, and it will be incredibly difficult, if not impossible, to turn around. Think about the situation of a cheating partner. This violation of trust, in which almost all barriers have been dropped, is all too common case. The sense of betrayal lingers, and at best, a semi-amicable parting may be the only possible short-term outcome. Even when such a relationship is repaired, there are generally cracks where there weren't any before. The betrayed partner is always looking for another instance of that trust being violated.

In the case of a business relationship, this kind of violation can often lead if not to criminal and civil legal battles, but for the one who broke the trust rapport, their reputation and ability to work successfully in that field could be ruined. Worse yet, it is getting creating a negative trust relationship where someone is trusted to do something wrong.

There was a very large, private company and some of the executive searches were incredibly complex with very esoteric skills requirements, and this was before taking into account the candidates' personalities. At this company, there was a member of the team who's father had a successful recruiting company, and this individual traded on their father's reputation. Whenever the team member received assignments, they did little to no work on them and had numerous excuses for why they couldn't find the right person or frequently passed on resumes of people who had applied but weren't qualified.

After a while, the team member got a reputation. They could be trusted to only put in a minimal amount of work while giving excuses. This eventually led to the team member drawing the wrong kind of attention.

Trust is something, once built, to be nurtured and protected. This \level is where the intersection between professional/ transactional connections and personal connections begins to blend and leads to higher levels of rapport, such as level six, which is identification = affinity/affiliation/admiration/affection.

# Chapter 14
# Level 6 – Identification = Affinity/Affiliation/Admiration/Affection

This level is different because there are four parts to it, unlike the other ones, and these have to do with gradations within the level and the amount of interaction that exists between the parties. This is a level where the parties may not know each other personally, and the rapport may seem one-sided, but it exists in that there is nonetheless an exchange where value exists.

In this case, the rapport has more to do with levels of identification that one side has with another. It can be in the form of a group or an individual. At this level, there is a need that is filled on a personal level for the person who is in rapport. If that person is seeking rapport with a leader of some kind, spiritual, business, sports, or entertainment, through identification, that person wants to take on the characteristics of that leader.

This is how sports teams can sell so many team jerseys, hats, and just about anything else with a team's logo and the name of a popular player on it. It is how entertainers can get thousands of fans to wait on line for tickets for a concert or how political figures can start movements that can change the course of nations. On a smaller level, this is also the area of influencers on social media. The admiration that these influencers garner is really about people identifying with them or their lifestyle with no regard for who the object of their identification is. This is also why people want to hear gossip about celebrities because their idols become human, making it easier with which to identify.

To influence with this type of rapport — identification — it is vital to be able to provide value for the people you want to influence to the extent that you overcome the boundaries that exist at the other levels. This is the area where you take your understanding of boundaries that you gained at the trust level, and you build those boundaries into what and how you are presenting information on a broader scale. This creates a self-selecting system for people to be influenced by you or not, and as long as you concentrate on those those boundaries you have described in the previously completed written exercise, you will be able to influence these groups.

This is also the level of rapport where cults are formed — cults of personality, religion, and celebrity or brand worshippers. At this level, people are seeking connection, validation, and affirmation. They are not someone who is alone or isolated; instead, they are part of a great whole, and they will be willing to sacrifice themselves and others in the cause of this greater whole.

We can see this in history. People who are yearning for something they can connect to — a lifestyle, type of celebrity who is living the life they want, etc. — live vicariously through others, or join a cause to give their lives more significant meaning. They want to identify with something other than themselves.

This identification has strong elements of that one-way rapport we described earlier as an obsession in that it is not returned directly but through indirect means. It is when the object of identification speaks and acts in a way that resonates with a person who is dissatisfied with their life and is looking for something new, then that is where a powerful connection is made. People have been known to alter their appearance to look like their favorite celebrity in their attempt to transform themselves.

Let's be very clear; this is not the same as having a role model from whom you learn lessons from their successes and failures. That said, you can easily see where this kind of rapport can lend itself to manipulation, and the well-publicized lawsuits and arrests in the news clearly illustrate this phenomenon.

But since we're talking about rapport for influence and persuasion being forewarned is forearmed, and knowing how it can be used maliciously is an excellent way to protect yourself. Now let's get into how to use it positively because there are many aspects of this where it can and is used positively. The first is in the area of leadership.

It is hard to lead if you don't have followers. If people do not:

i. have resonance with your message (affinity),
ii. feel like your message includes them (affiliation),
iii. don't admire you and who you are i.e., your values don't coincide with theirs,

you won't get past the trust level with them, and if they are distracted by qualities they find un-attractive, it is a barrier to identification.

All of these can be overcome when you are concentrating on global things that you have in common with the people you want to identify with you. Like attracts like, and so when you speak to more universal boundaries, you shift awareness, attention, respect, trust away from the common, day-to-day concerns to something much more global. This is an area for generalities in which the person being influenced fills in the blanks and forms the attachments with the person leading.

When you begin to tap into areas such as culture, trends, and beliefs, you have a robust current going in a direction that you can either ride or swim against. If you want to go against popular culture, it is a very long road, and it is much easier to find where there are wants and needs and go with them. When you are the first or the most articulate voice that is presenting solutions, even if you are not innovative, as the first person to bring attention to a problem and propose a solution, you are positioning yourself as a leader who others will want to identify.

Here's the secret to riding this current and catching a wave. You have to be the first to lower your boundaries. Remember all those boundaries you have identified and built over the previous levels, you have to be prepared to lower them. Now, this does not mean that your life becomes an open book. What happens is that you have to be prepared to open yourself to scrutiny and lower boundaries in areas that people typically would not – your life becomes public to a great extent.

This is the continuing secret of maintaining celebrity status, and we have seen this phenomenon rise over the years with reality television, shows like Big Brother, where people voyeuristically watch what happens during usually private interactions. This willingness to reveal oneself is how people gain followers on social media. People reveal aspects of their lives that they usually would never share. For people to identify with you, you have to give them things to identify with and to be able to influence and persuade at this level.

Exercise #1 – Get Naked

Here we are not talking about taking off your clothes; you can think of it as an analogy for what is happening.

1. Go back to your list of boundaries, and as you review them, mark off the ones that you are not only willing to reveal but are also willing to talk about, defend and hold no matter who tells you that you are wrong. This is not about the boundaries that you have; this is about the ones you are willing to reveal. In short, you are exposing yourself – getting naked.

2. Find out how these boundaries that you are willing to expose fit in with the culture you are in, or a trend you would like to be part of, or something that appeals to you that you want to publicize. It could be a cause; it could be something for which you are passionate.
3. Craft your message based on the words and phrases that are being used within these sub-communities. It is very much like you were doing in the earlier exercises except that instead of tailoring your message to a person or small group, it is to a large one.
4. Your message cannot just be the standard slogan the rest of the people who are interested in this popular current are spouting. It needs to be something that is your interpretation of the situation, and you have to stand by it – this is how you show leadership.
5. Because you have decided to stand out, you have to be prepared to defend your position. It doesn't have to be a radical defense at all; just know that you have to defend your position no matter what, or weakness will quickly destroy your position.
6. Know when to speak and when not to say anything – especially when you want others to fill in the blanks about yourself.

**Drew's Story**

When Drew got back from his exchange student year and rejoined our secondary school class, there was a genuine change in how he held himself, how he dressed, and how he interacted with people. It wasn't like he somehow became a punk rocker overnight because he certainly didn't, but he did show up with a very different, European flair.

Drew would never confirm, deny, or even comment on any of his peers' questions about relationships or sexual encounters and experiences. They even resorted to questioning his sexuality when he wouldn't talk about any of those aspects during his trip. What he did when asked, would look at them and smile with a distinct "I know something you don't" look in his eye like he remembered a pleasant memory.

This did far more to increase his reputation than bragging about any sexual conquest real or imagined ever could.

**Application**

Knowing when to talk and when to be quiet is an incredibly powerful form of influence and persuasion, and this leads to people projecting their own ideas on to you which, when positioned as Drew did, these people will identify with what they have projected onto you. You become a reflection of their aspirations and desires, and this is what celebrities have done through the ages. In secondary school, Drew did not take advantage of this but did enjoy a subtle form of the celebrity where one didn't exist before.

Because of this projection, when you can position yourself the way Drew did and then interject your viewpoints, these viewpoints will resonate with the people who have already created an affinity for you through their identification, and these viewpoints will be thought of as speaking what they are thinking.

Over time this affinity and affiliation, when it is in the form of a group, will lead to affection. The type of attachment will become stronger and seem more personal and, in doing so, can be passed on to others such as father to son or mother to daughter or any similar combination similar to how sports teams are often followed fanatically by generations of a family or political parties have generational membership, and it is the basis of all good branding.

*Influential Rapport*

If you buy a luxury brand, you will have a particular type of lifestyle, or that's what the subtle promise says. If you purchase a product endorsed by a celebrity, you will have a piece of that celebrity's lifestyle because that is what they also use – regardless of the truth of the matter.

Being able to adjust your boundaries and make no excuses for what you present behind them is a powerful attractor to people who are looking for something in their life, and when you do it, you create tremendous rapport and leverage for influence and persuasion.

Exercise #2 – Identification

1. Pick someone in the spotlight to study – it could be a celebrity, a politician, or sports star – and make it someone that is very well known outside of the influence category because this will require some research to outline how that person leveraged lowering their boundaries into their current position.
2. Was that person involved in a scandal? In something heroic? In something admirable? Do your research here from the earliest mentions to contemporary accounts. Scandals are generally the easiest to research and have the broadest and most frenzied coverage.
3. Chart out how that person handled the scandal in which they were involved. Was there an apology, or was there an attempt to play the victim? How did what they do affect the outcome? It is essential here to restrain yourself from passing judgment because your opinion on what happened in the past won't change anything, and what we are interested in is what the result was and how that person got there.
4. Do this for one person who survived a scandal and became a bigger celebrity either despite or because of this. Do the same for a person who did not survive a scandal.

5. Note the difference in how these situations were handled. If there were apologies involved, did they come from a position of strength or repentance?
6. Once you have done this for the world of celebrity, look at people in politics and do the same thing. You will notice patterns that you will be able to use and adapt to your situation.

# Chapter 15
# Level 7 – Love

**Drew's Story**

I got back into contact with Drew via social media. One day out of the blue, I received a friend request from him and accepted. We decided to meet up for coffee and to catch up after he said he had seen some of my videos and wanted to ask me about some things. Drew had a successful career, having finished college, graduated with an MBA, and joined a large technology company where he had a steady climb up the corporate ladder. Subsequently, he began moving from one company to another, always in a larger and more prestigious role. All was going well with his career, but never seemed to find that same easy success in his personal life. When he reached forty, he saw his climb slow, and he began to wonder why what had been so easy earlier on was now a struggle.

Before, he had been promoted every year and a half or so. He had kept up a string of semi-serious relationships, but there was always something missing. He kept an eye out for new career opportunities, but he always seemed to be a silver medalist with the latest and elevated roles going to someone else. He had just lost out on one of those roles, which would have taken him to the Vice President level in his company – a logical next step in his career progression. The feedback he received when told he didn't get the job was that he just wasn't quite the right fit for where that business needed to go.

At the same time, he had decided that his current relationship was getting serious, and he asked his girlfriend, Deirdre, to move in. After saying she would think about it, she abruptly broke off their relationship, telling him that his invitation was coming out the blue and that she had no idea he felt that way about her.

When I met him, he still had that same quiet charm he had developed in secondary school. There was that same look in his eye as if he knew something you didn't and that there was a private joke that you weren't in on. I could see why he had been successful, and at the same time, something was bothering him. After settling in with small talk, I mentioned that it was great to see him and catch up, but there was clearly something he wanted to talk about if he wanted to meet in person rather than just having a call or a video conference.

Drew went silent for a minute, looking at his coffee as if trying to put together his words. After all, it wasn't as if we were close friends, and we hadn't seen each other since secondary school, so in the sense of our adult lives, we were almost strangers.

He took a deep breath and told me about how he had been getting promoted regularly until recently and that his relationship that he thought was developing into something serious had broken up. He then told me that there were rumors that the company he was with was going to be merging with one of their biggest competitors and that there would be large scale redundancies, which was a nice word for layoffs. It is like all of sudden, having reached this level of success, everything was going wrong.

Drew said that he had read my books and seen my videos and had used some of the things I had taught successfully, so when he found me on social media, he decided to reach out to get some advice.

He told me how he had built his career, how he had come up with new plans which garnered attention at his company, how he had resisted pressures to compromise his values while finding solutions, and how he had built something of a following inside the company by forming a loyal team. This team was so loyal to him that the team had moved with him from company to company. Lately, however, those people were leaving his team for bigger jobs, and while he kept in touch and considered them close friends, the new people he brought on didn't have that same bond.

He went on to explain his relationship with Deirdre and how that had ended so abruptly. He also explained how he had come in second for another, more impressive job. He wondered if he had gotten as far as he was going to go?

When I asked him some of the questions about how he had built the loyalty of his team, he told me that he had consistently protected the team members from company politics, having them concentrate on performing at the highest level. He engineered ways for them to gain exposure within the companies they worked at, building a tremendous amount of trust, and he made sure to mentor them in his way of doing things. "That way, we all rise together, and we have even built a kind of brand," he proudly stated. He continued to tell me about the brand that he had built and the kind of results they achieved.

"Would you change that brand if you had to?" I asked with interest.

I could see the inner conflict he had with that question, but he replied, "I would, but that would be a last resort. Funny, the executives interviewing me asked a similar question."

Then I asked him about his relationship with Deirdre, a highly successful attorney with a great career. They seemed to hit it off immediately when they'd first met and had built their relationship in a way that accommodated their careers, and it had seemed smooth sailing for a year and a half. They were able to concentrate on their careers, but when they were together, they made sure to block the outside world out.

I was impressed that Drew was so open about his concerns and confusion about his life. So I asked him, "It seems that you are very close with the people on your team, and I am wondering, what stopped you from talking it over with the people you are close with on your team and with Deirdre? I appreciate you coming to me based on what you have seen of my work, but we haven't seen each other since secondary school?"

Drew just looked in his coffee for a moment and said, "I don't really know. I've always wanted to protect the team from the company politics so they could continue to focus on achieving great results, and people were attracted by the way we did things and the team brand we built. But it seems there are a lot of people who are doing the same kind of thing now, but we were first."

"OK," I said. "And what stopped you from telling Deirdre how you were feeling about your relationship?"

"She was ready a while ago, but I guess I wasn't ready to move things that far before," he answered. "I've always felt the need for some personal space."

For me, things were starting to become apparent. The things that had made Drew so successful earlier on – his ability to be **aware** of others and the effect he had on them, his ability to focus his **attention** on people and attract **attention** to himself, his ability to maintain command **respect** and give it in return and his ability to share enough of himself with his team to get them to **identify** with him and his brand at a deep level – were the things that were not holding him back professionally and personally.

"Drew," I said, "I appreciate that you want to talk to me about this, and I can help you, but you won't like how I do it."

"If it is a matter of payment," he said, "I do really well, so don't worry about that."

"It is not that," I replied. "We're going to have a chat about love."

He seemed taken aback by that and replied, "Well, if you can help me patch things up with Deirdre, that would be great, but I really came to you to talk about my career."

"It all comes down to the same thing, Drew," I said. "It all comes down to love.

"What do you mean?" he asked.

"In this case, it is about what you will do for your team out of **love**. Your decisions are influenced by your love for your team, so they know that will affect your decisions regarding the team, and you would be resistant to anyone persuading you to go a different way that might hurt the team. Also, when you are talking about the team as a brand, that shows you are identifying with your own brand, not the one that the company is promoting. You are only showing them what you want to show them, which is your brand.

"The feedback for my last interview, which was for a job I didn't get, was that I could do better with authentic leadership, but they weren't really clear about what that meant," remarked Drew.

"Authentic leadership," I smiled. "I've heard that one before. Love is about lowering boundaries which you have with your team, but you haven't built that kind of relationship with the people you would be working with in the new company who aren't on your team. In a very real sense, instead of lowering boundaries with them, you are showing them that they are on the other side of those boundaries. Leadership is also about lowering boundaries, and while you are showing them, you can do this with your team, they are getting the impression that you are focusing on that rather than on the wider team. With a more prominent role, there are more people and more layers."

Drew thought about that for a few minutes, sipping his coffee and staring into space. I could see that he was replaying his last interview in his mind.

He finally acknowledged, "I guess I could see that. I probably should have talked about how I like to build a team and my style of leading a team in a way that brings more people into it rather than talking about the team I would be bringing over."

"That would be a good start," I confirmed. "It is also about willing to be vulnerable, not showing them only the Drew brand."

"And what about Deirdre?" he asked.

"It seems like you had a comfortable relationship going," I suggested.

"Yes, we did. But then when I asked her to move in, she broke it off," he muttered.

"So, for over a year, you set boundaries for when she had wanted to talk about moving in at the time, but you weren't ready, and suddenly you wanted to drop them?" I asked.

"It is not that simple," he retorted. "My life was different back then, and things were going really well."

"And now?" I asked, taking a sip of my coffee.

"So what you are saying is that I wanted to change the boundaries, but she's not ready?"

## Influential Rapport

"I am saying that at the love level, it is the lowering of boundaries to form new ones with this person, not just lowering them and saying, "Here I am." In other words, when you lower yours, you have to be aware if she is ready to lower hers and make something new together. When she was ready, you weren't, and when you were ready, she wasn't. It sounds like you dropped the idea on her, and it could seem that it was out of frustration with what has been happening professionally rather than being about your relationship with her. Since you didn't let her in on your frustrations with your work life and how you are really feeling, she could only go by what she could observe. With the people closest to you, in this case, Deirdre, you have to drop both boundaries."

"I guess I should go talk to her then," Drew said, getting up from the table. "Thanks, I'll let you know how it goes."

"Before you go, I brought you something," I said, taking a book out of my bag and handing it to him. "This is my new book. It is a workbook on evolving your boundaries as you hit different stages in life. Remember, everything in using the rapport levels for influence and persuasion comes down to persuading yourself first."

Drew took the book and flipped through it. "Thanks, maybe I'll read it before I make any moves."

## Application

The most powerful and profound level of rapport, love, is where boundaries, while possibly not lowered, are, in many cases, ignored. And, it is when they are not ignored that the rapport bond is the strongest and can be shaken and possibly broken when adversity in other forms often makes the rapport stronger.

This is the level where trust is paramount, and identification is at its highest. This is why in marriage ceremonies, individuals are tied together as "one," and at its highest level, boundaries are reformed around the participants to serve as a way of binding these individuals together. This could be in the form of a couple, or it could be a team, and so it isn't the number of people that are important in this union but the act of bonding in itself.

There is a strong element of creating a new identity at this level. Where in the identification level you are filling in those areas found lacking when identifying with a person or entity, here you are forming a new one that encompasses and is shaped by this rapport level and the relationship within it.

This love overrides the individuality of a person, creating something that goes beyond identification. It propels someone to sacrifice their life for a spouse, children, comrades, and country because that individual is a genuine part of something greater.

When leveraging the love level in persuasion and influence, it is this appeal to sacrifice and preservation of the greater relationship that will move an individual to act and, in this case, selfless action. The focus is on the greater relationship – the person or entity who means more to the person who loves than their individual wellbeing.

While the expression of love is often more of a declaration of passion, that is just one aspect of love. It is powerful but, in many cases, short-lived. Like a sprint, it is fast, exciting, and can be fleeting. And it is often in these cases of passion that we learn how to lower our boundaries, or in the case of an early romance not going well, we learn not to lower them to our later detriment.

This is why love is, at the same time, the most potent, and dangerous rapport level because you are exposing yourself to a level that frightens many people. Being willing to let people inside your boundaries and then create new ones is the basis of the deepest of relationships, great teams, how societies are born, and how civilizations endure. When those boundaries are no longer respected, the relationships, teams, society, or civilization ultimately die from within.

It is best to know when love is being used as leverage in influence and persuasion, so rather than acting purely from emotion, realize when you are being manipulated. This area is where the worst acts of betrayal can take place, and there's any manipulation here should take into consideration the greatest of consequences.

When you appeal to love, it is always best to operate from the standpoint of doing what is in the best interest of the person you are attempting to persuade – acting from love. And when you do that, you will build deep rapport with the other person that could then lead to life-long loyalty.

# Chapter 16
# What Got You Here Will Keep You Here

## Creative Disruption

**Drew's Story**

    Drew took a long walk after leaving the coffee shop, wandering through New York as he made is way back uptown to his apartment on the upper east side. Usually, he would have just hailed a cab as the day was rapidly getting colder, but the wind cutting down the avenues seemed welcoming. He hadn't taken this type of walk since he had been in secondary school when he would sometimes walk just to get in some exercise before getting home and hitting the books.

    As he walked, he began going over his recent discussion and thought about the seven levels of rapport. When he was younger, it all seemed so natural. He had gone to the Netherlands and spent a magical year there, and he appeared to be able to make these connections quickly. Then after the years went by, and he had more success, he had actually put together the Drew brand and built a handpicked team that he had coached and led, which had led to even more success.

    But somewhere along the line, the "brand" got in the way. He had lived it for so long that he could see that he was always selling his brand. When he crossed 34th Street, he saw a couple walking the other way, holding hands and walking in step, synchronized. The way they moved, every so often looking deeply into each others' eyes, showed the level of rapport that they shared. It was corny, and he wondered if he and Deirdre had ever looked like that to other people.

No, he decided, they hadn't. They were never that in touch with each other, and even though Deidre would often take his hand while they were walking together, he could never really feel that connected. Hadn't he bought her expensive gifts to show her how he felt? They were like everything he liked associated with his life, quality, and luxury. She had often remarked that he could have just bought her flowers and not spent the money.

Drew walked up Fifth Avenue, the famous avenue where all the best brands could be found. He identified with them. He liked how they made him feel, and he liked his own brand. Identification – they were talking about identification earlier in the coffee shop. As he walked up the street, he noticed several of the old neighborhood stores that had been there for years were now closed, unable to deal with online competition, and he suddenly shivered as realization washed over him.

He had been living like those old stores, not adapting to the times. He had been relying on what had got him there in the past. Sure, people liked what he had done and wanted to be like him, but did they want to be him anymore? Looking back on how his life was going and mostly how alone he felt walking up Fifth Avenue, he wasn't sure he wanted to be like him anymore.

As he continued walking home, he began thinking about those boundaries that he was used to be lowering – those parts of himself that he liked to reveal because of how they reflected on him. He also thought of those things he had revealed to Deirdre, and more importantly, those things he hadn't.

When he got to his house, he went to the cabinet, pulled out a bottle of expensive whiskey, and almost poured himself a drink. Drew stopped and took a good look at the expensive liquor and realized that he didn't want a drink. He had to be clear-headed for what he knew he had to do.

## Application

Every obstacle is also an opportunity to reevaluate where you are in life, and if you are on the right track and when these obstacles start happening over and over, look for a pattern, and if there is one, it is time to do something different.

With your list of boundaries, now is an excellent time to take it out to reexamine– especially if you haven't done it in a while. Are these still working for you? Are you getting what you want out of them? Reexamining them periodically not only reminds you of what is working in your life and reinforcing those things that are working but is an opportunity to change directions if necessary.

Drew had fallen into a pattern where he had built up all the levels of rapport below love. When he got to identification, where his success accelerated, he became comfortable there. He tried to use it in every area of his life, not noticing that he had outgrown that level. By examining his boundaries, he could see that the ones he lowered to let people identify with him weren't the ones that were important as he progressed in his life and career. People weren't buying into his brand anymore, and he either had to develop a new brand or make an even more radical move.

The choice is to continue to evolve or and disrupt yourself or get disrupted out. After all, there are a lot of hungry, energetic younger people looking for opportunities to grow. Because this is about leadership, not following the latest trends, the obstacles are much more internal. In your life and career, you have theoretically gained experience at all the previous levels of rapport, but it is in taking the final step that the choice is presented. Are you comfortable enough with yourself to shift your boundaries, change and evolve what you have worked on over the years?

Remember, this is a choice. You don't have to take this step and could find a way to be happy with what you have. But to truly master all seven levels of rapport and be able to leverage them for influence and persuasion, you have to give yourself the choice of when, how, and to whom you open up totally. Updating where your boundaries are and what they are doing for you is the first step in this final process.

## Drew's Story

Drew emailed his boss that night saying that he wouldn't be in the next day. It would take him a little while to go through the workbook, and he sat down with a cup of coffee, skimming through the chapters. He could see where he was doing things successfully, and he remembered back to his secondary school days when he first began to develop his ability to gain rapport with people.

It hadn't been natural for him, but by observing and taking a few chances, he had noticed patterns in how people reacted to him and how he could influence them by opening up to them, shifting his barriers when appropriate. At first, he had been very conscious of how much he could let people in, and that worked well for him. As he became more successful, he was able to build a persona that he could be open about with people and that had accelerated his success.

But was that really him? The more successful he got, the more he began to suspect they were identifying with the persona he had constructed so carefully over the years. Was that really him, and wasn't that the person everyone wanted? As he thought back on his life and choices, he noticed that he was always cautious about what he said and presented to the world. When he was happy, he never had a problem sharing that with others, but when disappointed or angry, he made sure no one ever saw it – not his parents and definitely not Deirdre.

As he meditated on his life, he noticed that the boundary he built around his private self had gotten stronger and stronger over time, and his public self was all he was allowing anyone to see. This dynamic had become stronger and stronger as the stakes became higher, with each success and each relationship to the point where he wasn't comfortable with revealing his private self to anyone.

As he continued to ponder his situation, he tried to think back to the last time he was truly himself. There were glimpses of that self when he was alone in the mornings, getting ready for work or when he was sitting at home alone, but when he interacted with someone else, it seemed his other side would jump to the front, and it was just easy to let that part of him take over.

He opened his new book to the love section and read through the first paragraph: "To operate ethically at the love level, you have to be willing to accept others for who they are, the good and bad parts." Pretty standard stuff, he thought as he read on: "To do that, you have to first love those good and bad parts about yourself." "Okay," thought Drew. "Easier said than done."

He leafed forward to the section that read, "Exercise – Introducing You To You."

## Application

Exercise #1 – Introducing You To You

For this exercise to work, you have to be prepared to be absolutely honest with yourself. You can choose to write down what you come up with, or you can make a list in the privacy of your mind; it is up to you. Remember, the more honest you are with yourself, the more progress you will make.

1. Sit back and close your eyes. Take a deep breath and allow yourself to relax.
2. Imagine yourself standing entirely naked, looking out of your own eyes.
3. Once you are comfortable standing there alone, step out of your body and walk forward three steps, turn around and look at yourself without criticism.
4. There are probably parts of yourself that you don't think are as attractive as you would like them to be and other parts that you are proud of and other features that you think could be improved – just look at yourself and take them in.
5. Once you have had a chance to really look at yourself, look at the first thing you aren't happy about and ask yourself – why? Are you judging by your standards or someone else's, and is that a reasonable standard? After you know whose standard you are using, are you willing to accept that part of yourself and, if necessary, do something about it, and if so, what?
6. Repeat that process with every part you are not happy with, being absolutely honest with yourself. If you are judging by someone else's standards, then substitute your standards, and you can plan to make improvements if that is what you want
7. After you have done this process for the parts of yourself you are not happy with, do this with the features that you are satisfied with and see if you want to make any improvements.
8. Now there will likely be parts that you accept as perfectly fine, and you are neither happy nor unhappy with them but accept them for what they are with no improvement needed. Notice these parts and your feelings about them. Are you judging by other peoples' standards or your own?
9. Notice if there is a pattern of you judging yourself by others' standards. If you are doing that in important areas, it may be challenging to shift or evolve your boundaries to the point necessary to access the love rapport level.

10. Now that you know which areas you would like to improve, create your standards by asking yourself what is important for you about that area and create that list as you did previously in examining your boundaries.
11. Once you have done this, open your eyes and take a short break. Then notice how different you feel now that you are creating new standards for yourself. Notice how that affects your willingness to shift your boundaries because once you have done that, you will be disrupting yourself out of your zone of comfort.

Exercise #2 – Creating Your Disruption

To disrupt yourself, you have to know in what direction you would like to go. After reviewing your boundaries and having that clearly in mind, continue with these steps.

1. Think about how you would like your life to be and imagine yourself standing on a line where the future stretches before you, and the past is behind you.
2. In front of you are your goals, the things you want in life. Line them up in an order that makes sense to you. For example, if you want a new house or a new car, it would help to have a way to pay for it first. Add color to these things that you want; this color will help you identify these things on your timeline.
3. After you have added color to the things you want in life, add blocks of color that represent your boundaries and notice if the things you want in life are in line with your boundaries. How are those boundaries helping you or hindering you in getting what you want? Chances are, when the boundaries are hindering you, they will be standing between you and your goals and if they are helping, they'll be acting as channels to help lead you to your goals.

4. Now that you know which ones are hindering you, you can choose to either drop your goals or shift your boundaries
5. Experiment with shifting or lowering you're a boundary that is blocking one of your goals. Does it help you get what you want, and are you comfortable with not having that boundary there? Remember also to look farther forward to see what would happen and who you would be without that boundary.
6. If you decide to drop a boundary, is there one that would be better for you and the life you want to have? If so, insert that new boundary and look forward and see what kind of life you could have
7. Repeat this step with every boundary that is blocking a goal and notice how your life could be different
8. Once you have these new boundaries, look back at your past and notice if your experiences and feelings about your past have changed.
9. Once you have reviewed your past, look forward again and see what the first step is that you should take to achieving your goals. Move that step closer to you until it feels possible and decide on how long you will give yourself to take action. Then notice what the next step should be and the step after that until you achieve your goal. You might appreciate that there are some things on there that you hadn't thought about and there are some things that you don't have to do. Remember, this is your way of designing the rest of your life
10. Once you have your plan of action, open your eyes and notice how you have changed the way you feel about opening up a new path for yourself.
11. Close your eyes again and notice what would happen with your life when you are able to lower your barriers whenever you want because the barriers are there to protect you, but at what point does a protected place become a prison?

12. Imagine being able to fully show yourself to another person, to be able to trust fully, to be able to identify with each other, and accept each other and, therefore, to love.
13. Close your eyes again and imagine your timeline with your goals and new boundaries laid out in front of you. Imagine how your life would be with this new ability to drop your boundaries whenever you decide to. See how that would change your life and when you have that, imagine times in the past where this ability would have changed your life and see how different those experiences would have been
14. Now back in the present with these new abilities go into this new phase of your life knowing you can always come back and adjust anything on your timeline that you want

Taking the time to examine your boundaries periodically will be a useful exercise in making sure that they fit with your current lifestyle and circumstances. If you are still behaving in the same way that you were when you were a teenager and you are in your thirties, you can easily understand how that kind of operating mode might not be the best way to be living your current life.

In addition to examining how your boundaries are working for where you are in life, it will also allow you to adjust them for where you want to be so you can make a smooth transition to the next stage of your life. Mastering the ability to shift your boundaries and bring people into your world wholly and honestly will be the key to being able to use the love level of rapport ethically in influence and persuasion.

# Chapter 17
# Bringing It All Together

**Drew's Story**

Drew looked up from the menu when Deidre entered the quiet restaurant. It was a weekday evening, so it wasn't crowded, and they would have some privacy. He put down the menu and stood up and shared a brief hug and a kiss before holding her seat for her as she sat down.

"On your best behavior tonight, I see," she said with a smile. "You stopped doing that about six months into our relationship."

"Let's just say I've been doing a lot of reflecting on the past," he offered.

The waiter came up to the table and asked if they wanted to order drinks, leading to a surprised look on Dierdre's face.

"You usually order for me," she said, "I'm surprised you waited."

"It occurred to me that I never really asked you what you wanted, I just noticed that you usually ordered the same thing, but I never checked to see if you ever wanted anything other than red wine."

Deirdre smiled warmly, "That's something new. So it calls for something new. How about iced tea?"

"Of course, ma'am," replied the waiter, "And you sir?"

"Something new for me too. I'll have the same. But I think we'll need a few minutes to look at the menu."

The waiter went off to get their drinks, and they settled into an uncomfortable silence.

The waiter returned with their drinks, and they raised a quick toast, "Cheers," they said simultaneously.

"So, I guess you're wondering why I asked you here," Drew asked in a lousy imitation French detective accent.

Deidre tried to stifle a laugh at this unexpected opening and smiled, "I was a bit surprised, I'll admit. But I did think I would hear from you, maybe in another few days or so. It was a week the last time we fought."

He smiled back at her. "I've been doing a lot of thinking and making some changes in my life. I resigned from the company and worked out a separation agreement – I guess since they are going into a merger, they would have gotten rid of me anyway."

"Really," Deidre said. "That is a surprise. So what are you going to do now? I know you have been interviewing, so I am sure something new will come up."

"Actually," he said, "I am making bigger changes than that. I've been doing a lot of soul searching and have come to some conclusions. There are some things about myself that I haven't take the time to think about in a long time. Basically, I've been doing the same thing on bigger scales for so long that I haven't taken the time to reevaluate my life, and that includes our relationship."

"Really?" she said, "I thought we broke up?"

"If truth be told, I think you broke up with me. I haven't accepted yet," he smiled. It was a different smile than the one she had been used to seeing. "It is all part of what's been going on, really. Remember I told you the feedback I got from my last interview? They said that I didn't score well in authentic leadership?"

"I remember," she said. "And then you asked me to move in with you."

"You didn't seem surprised. Not about the moving in part because I think I did surprise you there, but about the authentic leadership piece."

Deidre took a deep breath and took a sip of her iced tea. "Well, if I am being honest, then no. I think you do a great job, and your team thinks the world of you. It is just that you seem so concerned about them and they of you, that it is like there's a bubble around you all, and it is hard to become a part of that. I know they would do anything for you and you for them, but from someone outside of that, it seems like they would always be a secondary consideration."

"Did I make you feel that way?" he asked, looking at her intensely.

"I know you never meant to," she said. "But it is like there's the you that's leading this team and that's the you I see all the time and still, I know there's more to you than that. I fell for that guy who's leading the team because I could tell there was more there. I know that part of you is in there even if you don't, and I didn't get to see it, so I couldn't move in with you since that part is a stranger."

Deidre expected him to deny it; he had done that other times when she tried to talk to him about being that person he shared with his team.

Drew smiled at her and looked her in the eyes and said, "You're right."

Deidre didn't react for a moment as she processed what he said, "I'm right?"

"Absolutely," said Drew. "That's what I've been thinking about and working on the last few days." He reached under the table to his backpack and pulled out the workbook his friend had given him at the coffee shop. "I've been reexamining my boundaries and how I use them to create rapport and realize I am really good at six levels of rapport, awareness, attention, respect, trust, and identification."

Deirdre smiled at him and said, "I guess you are. I am here."

"But I am not good at the highest level, love," he continued. "I am not talking about the emotion, you know I love you, but I am talking about love in rapport."

"What do you mean?" she asked.

"According to this, which was written by a friend of mine, rapport, especially in how you use it to influence and persuade, is about boundaries."

"OK, I can see that, I think," she said.

The waiter came by to see if they were ready to order, and they asked for a few more minutes.

"Well, everything that's happened in the last few days has forced me to take a look at myself and my boundaries and where I've dropped them," he looked at her meaningfully. "And where I haven't."

"So there really is that piece of you I haven't seen? Is he ready to come out and play?"

"I guess he is, the question is, will you want to play with him after you meet him?" he asked hopefully.

"We'll find out over dinner," Deidre smiled and waved the waiter over.

A year later, Drew was sitting in his new home office and looked out the French doors that led to the pool. It was another bright, sunny day in Tampa, where he had moved a few months after leaving his company. It had been a hectic year since leaving, and it had definitely not been easy at first.

Drew thought back to when he told his team about his decision. He called an all-hands team meeting and pulled everyone into the room. He began by telling them about the changes he had decided to make in his life, like leaving New York City where he had been born and raised, and leaving the company where they had been the top performers for the last three years.

Standing in front of the group, Drew announced, "After really reflecting on what we've achieved and what we've been able to do together across several companies, I realized one thing. We love each other, but I haven't been doing my part."

They began to object, but he raised his hands and said, "Please let me continue. I know you understand how I feel about all of you, and I would and have done everything I could to open the way for you to achieve everything we've done and add value to the company. What I haven't done is reciprocate enough to encourage you to spread your own wings.

"Sure, I've always given a great recommendation when one of the team has decided to accept other offers, but I realize that I shouldn't have just protected you because that's been holding you back from your own development as leaders. So I've decided to step back, and I'll support all of you as best I can, but I am doing you a disservice by not encouraging you to be the best at who you can be."

Naturally, the team was a bit worried about what would happen to them, but Drew knew that they all had the skills to do what they wanted, and he made a promise to them that he would help them clarify and achieve their own goals without their love for him standing in their way. This gave him more insight into how the love level influences and persuades even without intent behind it because it is so powerful that the intent is not necessarily coming from the object of the Love but from the person who Loves.

In his case, he Loved his team and wanted to protect them, but this led to being too protective, and he stifled their professional growth. In their case, they loved him, and so they sacrificed their growth for him, so great was their love and loyalty. By setting them free, he equalized the balance and dynamic between them and found that he no longer had to play corporate politics for them and himself.

The past year had been a year of growth and development for himself. He began to understand how to best leverage rapport at every level, and it led to not only better relationships but also his new business as a coach/consultant, and he began to be recognized as a thought leader in the area of authentic leadership, coaching executives on those areas where he had lacked a year ago.

Deirdre came into the room and sat down on his lap. She was just beginning to show her pregnancy, and they were planning an anniversary trip before travel got too difficult for her, but he had a few projects scheduled for right after they got back.

"What are you working on? I thought we were to go looking for baby stuff."

Drew smiled and pulled her close, "Just finishing the outline for the training I am going to be giving."

"Where is it this time?"

Drew smiled and showed her the deck he had been working on. It had the company's name on it.

"Isn't that the company that turned you down last year?" she asked with a laugh.

"Yep," he replied. "And it was the best thing that could have happened. Well, second-best, that is," he added with a smile. "I'll finish this later, let's go shopping for baby stuff."

**Application**

When at the love level of rapport, people can be easily manipulated through love. If barriers are down, there is no need for manipulation. People will be self-motivated to act based on the love they are feeling. The boundaries that would typically be there to protect an individual are dropped, and new ones extended around the people, organizations, or entities involved, and almost any action can be justified in a person's mind because of this.

Does this mean that we shouldn't access this level of rapport? Of course not. It is through love that some of the most outstanding achievements in history have happened, and the happiest moments in life occur. Having the facility to raise and lower these boundaries to gain perspective will allow you to figure out if you are acting in a way that exploits others or helps them get what they want in alignment with what you want. Always remember to routinely check where your Boundaries are and how they are interacting with other peoples'.

The love level is where through rapport, influence and persuasion is seamless because motivation is internal, and the person being influenced concludes that the direction they are going is their idea.

Exercise #1 Rapport at the Love Level

By going first, and lowering your boundaries, and showing your vulnerability, you are inviting the other person to really know you, and that creates an incredible bond.

1. Maintain this openness while interacting with this person and keep it going consistently because if you only open up sporadically, the other person will see it as an attempt to manipulate or, at best, a disingenuous attempt at making a connection.
2. When the other person begins to drop their boundaries in return, do not move forward quickly but continue to hold your boundaries in check while the other person explores who you are – this is potentially an uncomfortable time and the reason for the previous exercise in accepting yourself.
3. Go slow when exploring who the other person is and accept that person for who they are. If there are any areas where the other person is uncomfortable, resist the urge to go in and fix things. That is something you can discuss at a later date.
4. Begin to build new mutual boundaries around each other that will serve as a new basis for this shared rapport.

When this is done with groups, this process will take longer, and the person who is creating the rapport will have to hold their boundaries open longer, and there will be different nuances to each relationship within the whole. So I recommend using the exercise, Introducing You To You exercise regularly.

# Chapter 18
# Quick Start Guide

Putting Rapport Into Action

The key to making the seven levels of rapport work for you is in understanding which one of those seven levels you are operating on with yourself and where that corresponds in the person you want to influence. So here is a way to get started. This does not mean that you shouldn't do the other exercises outlined in the book; they are designed to increase your skills at every level, but this will help you begin to operate in the context of an overarching system of building and maintaining rapport through the levels.

The first step is to evaluate which level you are comfortable during your interactions. Gaining awareness of your own boundaries is the first place to start. Are you having an impact on others around you, positive or negative? Do they even notice your presence?

You might think that it is because their own awareness is limited, and while that might be the case, if it is a repeating pattern, then it is likely that your boundaries are drawn around you so tightly that the most outgoing and open person in the world won't be able to make a connection with you. Knowing where your comfort zone is will allow you to take action to expand it in order to use the next level of rapport. Following this progression will accelerate your progress through the seven levels and allow you to use them to influence in any situation.

Gaining knowledge of how you are influenced by these levels will give you insight and sensitivity in knowing how you can influence and persuade through the seven levels of rapport. By meeting people at whichever level they are at, you will quickly build and maintain rapport with others. Once you have rapport at one level, you will have the opportunity to move people into a higher level, thereby creating a stronger bond and more opportunity for influencing and persuading.

Quick Start Exercise - Awareness Level

1. Once you have found where your awareness boundary lies, you can take the next step to create rapport with people at that level. You can start by simply beginning transactional interaction with people. Smile at someone you don't usually have much interaction with, such as if you buy a cup of coffee, then smile at the person who takes the money and notice if that person smiles back. It is a natural reaction for people to smile when you smile at them.
2. The next step is as you approach someone, it doesn't have to be someone you will necessarily have interaction with, notice that the person will either raise their eyebrows or nod. This is something that is pretty universal among people and is a way of acknowledging your existence in their space. You are very likely doing one of them unconsciously yourself. Continue to notice this until it becomes comfortable for you.

Quick Start Exercise – Attention Level

1. After you become aware of how people are acknowledging your presence, use the same movement back when you see it. If the person raises her eyebrows to you, raise yours in return. If the person nods, then nod back, and as you do this, become aware of how close you can mirror that same movement and notice that the feeling between you begins to relax.
2. The next step is to do this with someone with whom you are going to have an interaction. It could be a cashier at the store, or it could be a server at a restaurant or even someone with whom you are working. And, if it is someone with whom you

have regular contact, notice how that interaction goes more smoothly.

## Quick Start Exercise – Respect Level

1. Once you have become comfortable with the previous exercises, and are creating rapport on the awareness and attention levels, notice the distance at which you stand when you are having an interaction with someone.
2. Once you have done this several times, you will notice that there is a certain distance at which you and the other person feel comfortable.
3. Notice what happens when you try to shorten that zone. Does that person remain relaxed, or does that person start to react and try to regain the distance?
4. While you are doing this, notice your comfort level by changing the distance. Do this slowly, and you will soon see and feel in a very visceral way the effect of respecting and not respecting a boundary.
5. This will be a jumping-off point for being able to elicit boundaries at the respect;level and increase your sensitivity while doing the exercises outlined in the respect chapter of this book.

## Quick Start Exercise – Affiliation Level

1. This exercise starts with observation, both of self and others. Take an inventory of the things with which you identify. Start at the smallest level and work your way up. Do you feel an affiliation for a particular group, whether it is ethnic, social, religious, etc.? Are you a member of a specific club, or do you identify yourself with a stratum of society? Are you affiliated with a political party? In any event, it is essential to understand where the affiliations are to move to the next step.

2. As you list these on a piece of paper, notice how they affect how you view life. For example, if you feel affiliation for a sports team and your team has a rival, how do you feel about that team and its fans? As another example, there are notable rivalries among the branches of the military due to their affiliations. How do you feel about them?
3. Notice how these affiliations affect your outlook on life and your opinions. These are invisible influences that have grown from being affiliated with these entities. It has been observed that if you spend all your time with unsuccessful people you are much more likely to be unsuccessful, and when you spend your life with successful people, you are more likely to be successful because these group viewpoints inform your view of the world.
4. Knowing that influences are there and that the leaders of these groups have an easier time persuading people who are affiliated with them allows you to observe, resist or use these influences when persuading others to do what you want. Some examples of how these can be used follow. Finish the sentences for your own perspective:

   a. A true fan would never_____.
   b. Are you a patriot or a traitor?

5. A compassionate person would always contribute ____. Think about your own examples and how they have been used to influence your thoughts and persuaded you to perform specific actions.

Please note, this is not necessarily a sinister, or manipulative phenomenon; it goes to the motive of the person who is leveraging it. Pure and impure motives can be put into action, and the outcomes can be similar. It is in having the interests of the person being influenced in mind versus the desires of the influencer that there is a divide between the two.

Quick Start Exercise – Identification Level

1. Think about what characteristics in your life you would like to improve; it could be how you interact with people, your willingness to meet others if you are shy, or it could be that you would like to be in better shape.
2. Find someone who embodies these characteristics that you want to have, it could be someone you know or someone you follow on television or social media, or it could be a character from a film.
3. When you have found that person, imagine that person embodying those characteristics that you identify with that person.
4. Once you have identified those characteristics, close your eyes and imagine a filter around yourself to screen out those characteristics of that person that you do not desire; for example, the person whose characteristics you identify with might be a smoker, so that's a characteristic you wouldn't want to adopt.
5. Once you have your filter in place, imagine that person who has these characteristics standing in front of you with their back to you. Consider details such as what the person is wearing and how they are breathing.
6. Go into a neutral state, a state where you leave behind any expectations and open yourself to merely experiencing what your life will be like with these new characteristics.
7. Step into this construct and open yourself up to receive the characteristics with which you identify. Experience how you would move through the world with these characteristics and bathe your neurology in this experience.

8. Think about scenarios in the past where you would have used these characteristics, for example, if you were shy before and instead were social. Consider if you were not motivated to work out, now when thinking about the exercise, how is your experience of the world different? Go through these scenarios one by one, knowing you can add or reduce parts of these characteristics to design your life and your experience.
9. When you have experienced these characteristics enough to be comfortable with them, step out of the construct that you had made and open your eyes, noticing how your experience of the world is changing.
10. When you go into new situations, allow yourself to act differently than you had previously known. You can always go back to the construct you created to get recharged, or you can create a new one with different or better characteristics.

Quick Start Exercise – Love Level

1. Sit in a quiet place where you won't be disturbed. Take a deep breath and close your eyes as you breathe out. Take another deep breath and tighten all of your muscles as much as you can for a count of ten and then relax them all at the same time.
2. As you feel your body relax, take another deep breath, and allow yourself to drift with your eyes closed.
3. Think about who you love; it could be your partner, your children, your family – what would you do to protect these people?
4. What would you do to make them happy? List them in your mind.
5. Once you are sure in your mind about what you would for who you love, think about what you love, it could be what you do for a living, it could be travel, it could be playing a sport.
6. Think about how that love motivates you to do things and what do you love about it. It could be that feeling of

achievement in your profession, and it could be seeing new places, it could be the feeling of well being and joy you have playing a sport – whatever it is, notice how that motivates you.

7. When you have that awareness, realize that in knowing how these things motivate you and move you to do something you love and protect and nurture your loved ones, you can then begin seeing how others are inspired by the people and things they love as well. This is the first step in gaining awareness of how to operate at the love level.

# Chapter 19
# Final Thoughts

The ability to build and maintain rapport is something that happens naturally as we are generally social creatures and live within society; however, dysfunctional it may seem at times. This original survival mechanism continues through to the modern-day precisely because it is necessary to gain if not friends, then allies to navigate our increasingly complex civilization. Throughout all the technological changes we have experienced, we still have the intense yearning for connection, not always in the sense of liking each other but that we can interact without conflict.

By learning the skills of rapport and understanding rapport is a process that can be moved through, we can fine-tune our ability to create these relationships. We can create them no matter how transactional they might be, to influence and persuade to our benefit and the benefit of those with whom we interact.

As a parting suggestion, I encourage you to work as best you can in the framework of what is right for both you and the other party. When operating solely in your interests, using these skills will get you what you want, but you will not be able to maintain the rapport you previously built. The betrayal of rapport, especially from the trust level up, is the easiest way to create enemies in your wake as you move through the world. When used with compassion, these skills will open opportunities to build a network of friends and allies. You will be able to leverage this network because you have already spread your influence to them and persuaded them that it is safe and to their advantage to interact with you.

Create rapport wherever you go and at whatever level is appropriate and enjoy a more prosperous and more successful life with these new skillsets.

**Other books by James Seetoo:**

*The 5 Keys To Hypnotic Selling*

For more resources, information on trainings and videos please go to:

https://jc2consulting.com

or visit my Facebook page at: https://www.facebook.com/jmseetoo

For more videos please visit my YouTube channel:

https://www.youtube.com/channel/UCKBxv0FCSkdqnYi8KzwLObg?view_as=subscriber

Made in the USA
Columbia, SC
22 March 2021